Establishing the Kingdom Series

THE KINGDOM FOUNDATIONS COURSE MANUAL

THE JOSHUA GENERATION

P.O Box 14472, 00100, Nairobi, Kenya
Telephone:+254-020-2605300
email: info@jgmail.org
www.thejoshuagenerationtrust.org

Making your God Given Vision a Reality

TABLE OF **CONTENTS**

INTRODUCTION

Karibu ("Welcome" in Kiswahili), to the Kingdom Foundations Course Manual.

This manual is a compilation of godly and scripture-based principles that will build and strengthen unshakable Kingdom foundations in your life. The principles taught in this book are profitable to the born again believer who desires fundamental building blocks of the Christian life and the Kingdom of God.

It is also suitable for those who have not yet accepted Jesus Christ as their personal Lord and Saviour, and would like to know more about the Christian faith.

This book can be used for personal and group study, for follow-up of new converts to Christianity and the Kingdom of God, for foundational and/or discipleship classes in churches and ministries (including Para-church organisations), in institutions of learning as part of the school curriculum, in estate or neighbourhood fellowships, in hospitals, in prisons ministry, as material for ministering at crusades and church services, for personal edification and daily ministration of the five-fold minister of the Gospel of the Lord Jesus Christ.

Whatever your need for this material might be, we pray that the content in this book will refresh, edify (build you up), encourage, and bring you comfort, even as it illuminates and strengthens your faith in God and His Kingdom. We pray it will help to further mature, equip, and position you to be the best that you can be for God all the days of your life.

Enjoy your study.

CHAPTER 1:

THE GODHEAD AND THE FATHER

Definition of the word "God"

The Oxford English dictionary defines the word "God" as "the creator and ruler of the universe. A super-being who is to be worshipped, and has power over nature and human affairs". Yet this definition is not sufficient and as such must be looked into from a more biblical perspective and depth.

The Bible Definition: The word "God" derived from both the Hebrew word "Elohiym" and the Greek word "Theos" simply means "a **Supreme Divinity or being**". It means "**a magistrate or judge** of all life forms". It also means "**a mighty or very great deity**".

1. God is therefore the creator of all life, and the Supreme Being over all creation. He is the father of all spirits as shown in Hebrews 12:9. He is divine (all-perfect and all-excellent). All creation was made by Him and for His purpose.

2. God is Judge over all His creation. To be a judge means to pronounce sentence (for or against), to vindicate or punish, to govern, to defend, to contend, to avenge, to rule, and to carry out or execute judgment.

3. God is a mighty or very great being, therefore meaning that God is Almighty, great (the greatness associated with deity), goodly, all powerful, and stronger than any other being.

The Trinity of God

The word "trinity" signifies the union of three Persons to make the GODHEAD, and this is namely, God the Father, God the Word (Son), and God the Holy Spirit. They are three, yet in perfect unity or oneness: one God, but three distinct Persons.

For there are three that bear record in heaven, the Father, the Word, and the Holy Ghost: and these three are one.

1 John 5:7

God is infinitely greater than man is and therefore there is a lot about Him that we cannot fully understand from our dimension of life. There are great truths about God that are beyond our comprehension yet they are not contrary to reason.

Such knowledge is too wonderful for me; it is high, I cannot attain unto it.

Some illustrations used as an analogy of the trinity of the Godhead

We can use certain physical analogies to explain the trinity of God because the scriptures say that we can understand the spiritual things of the Godhead from nature.

Because that which may be known of God is manifest in them; for God hath shewed it unto them.
For the invisible things of him from the creation of the world are clearly seen, being understood by the things that are made, even his eternal power and Godhead; so that they are without excuse:

Romans 1:19-20

Some of these analogies are:

1.The rays from the sun. The sun is one sun made up of the chemical energy (the actual fire burning in the sun), the heat waves, and the light rays. Yet the three are in unity and it is one sun.

2.The light bulb. It gives light, dissipates heat, and has electric current flowing through it all at once.

3.The constitution of man. Man is a spirit, possesses a soul, and lives in a physical body, yet the three parts of man work together as one.

And the very God of peace sanctify you wholly; and I pray God your whole spirit and soul and body be preserved blameless unto the coming of our Lord Jesus Christ.

1 Thessalonians 5:23.

4. A football. It consists of the outer leather, the inner bladder, and the air contained inside. Yet the three make up one football.

God the Father

God the father sits as the head of the Godhead or Trinity.

On numerous occasions in the gospels, we see either Jesus Christ referring to God as Father, during communication with Him, or while speaking to others.

Jesus saith unto him, I am the way, the truth, and the life: no man cometh unto the Father, but by me.

John 14:6

And now, O Father, glorify thou me with thine own self with the glory which I had with thee before the world was.

John 17:5

Jesus Christ introduced to us another name and position of God as our Father. He helped us come to a better understanding of the Trinity, and the name and ministry of God the Father. Jesus Christ introduced and revealed God as Father to mankind. He brought to us the revelation of God as Father.

And it came to pass, that, as he was praying in a certain place, when he ceased, one of his disciples said unto him, Lord, teach us to pray, as John also taught his disciples.
And he said unto them, When ye pray, <u>say, Our Father which art in heaven</u>, Hallowed be thy name. Thy kingdom come. Thy will be done, as in heaven, so in earth.

Luke 11:1-2

He also brought us into a place of relationship with God the Father whereby we can also call Him "Father", "our Father".

For ye have not received the spirit of bondage again to fear; but ye have received the Spirit of adoption, whereby <u>we cry, Abba, Father</u>.

Romans 8:15

But when the fulness of the time was come, God sent forth his Son, made of a woman, made under the law,
To redeem them that were under the law, that we might receive the adoption of sons.
And because ye are sons, God hath sent forth the Spirit of his Son into your hearts, crying, Abba, Father.
Wherefore thou art no more a servant, but a son; and if a son, then an heir of God through Christ.

Galatians 4:4-7

The word "**Abba**" used by Jesus in the scriptures is an Aramaic word. It is an intimate Aramaic word for "Father". It is the word framed by the lips of infants calling to their earthly father. It is a personal name a child calls the father, E.g. Daddy, Baba, Papa, etc. It expresses unreasoning trust by a child in the father.

TEST YOURSELF:
CHAPTER 1 – THE GODHEAD AND THE FATHER

The answer sheet is provided at the back of this manual.

1. What does the word "Elohiym" mean?

   a) The Lord of Hosts.
   b) A Supreme Divinity or being.
   c) The judge of some life forms.
   d) The God who prospers.

2. Who are the Persons that make up the trinity?

   a) The Arch-angels, God the father, and God the Holy Spirit.
   b) God the Word, God the Holy Spirit, and the twenty four elders.
   c) God the Father, God the Word, and God the Holy Spirit.
   d) None of the above.

3. Which of the following rightly describes the word Abba?

   a) It is a casual word describing a friend
   b) It is a name that a servant uses to refer to the master
   c) It is an intimate name used by a child to the father
   d) None of the above

4. God the father sits as the head of _____.

5. One of Jesus Christ's roles was to introduce and reveal _____
_____ to mankind.

CHAPTER 2:

THE KINGDOM OF GOD

Definition of a Kingdom

The word Kingdom comprises of two words: <u>King</u> and <u>domain</u>. They basically refer to a king's domain or area of influence. Further broken down this refers to the region, area, territory that is under the influence and /or authority of a King.

For there to be a Kingdom, there has to be a king (Leader) and a domain to be governed. This domain will be made up of a community of creatures (people and other living beings within that territory), some geography, resources, and a social system (E.g. School, markets, government, etc) in which this community interacts daily.

God's Kingdom

Of the increase of his government and peace there shall be no end, upon the throne of David, and upon his kingdom, to order it, and to establish it with judgment and with justice from henceforth even for ever. The zeal of the Lord of hosts will perform this.

Isaiah 9:7

God also has His Kingdom. This is the region, territory, people, geography, resources, and civilization which are under the rule, reign or influence of God as their King. The Kingdom of God spans over heaven, the universe, and the earth. God is meant to rule over all His works (creation of His hands).

Who is the image of the invisible God, the firstborn of every creature:
For by him were all things created, that are in heaven, and that are in earth, visible andinvisible, whether they be thrones, or dominions, or principalities, or powers: all things were created by him, and for him:
And he is before all things, and by him all things consist.

Colossians 1:15-17

God's Kingdom is above and greater than any other Kingdom in power, wealth, glory, and every other capacity. In essence, God is the creator of the heavens and the earth and all therein: therefore His Kingdom is vast and supreme. His Kingdom reigns over all other kingdoms and there is none at par with it. The scriptures clearly show that the whole earth, its inhabitants, its fullness, and even the heavens all belong to God (and are supposed to be under God's reign).

The earth is the LORD'S, and the fulness thereof; the world, and they that dwell therein.
For he hath founded it upon the seas, and established it upon the floods.

Psalm 24:1-2

Kingdom of darkness

Satan was once an angel created by God and called Lucifer. He was an angel that worshipped God but he allowed his positioning of glory in God's Kingdom to corrupt him and bring him into pride and rebellion to the sovereignty of God. He wanted to be equal to God and sit on the throne of God. He then became the first sinner and changed in nature from Lucifer an angel of God into Satan or the devil an accuser. His nature became sinful as a result of this act of treason towards God. He deceived and misled one-third of the angels in heaven to accompany him in his act of rebellion and sabotage. Yet they were unsuccessful and were all eventually cast out of heaven unto the earth. (Isaiah 14:12, Ezekiel 28:17-18, & Revelation 12:9).

Ever since then, the devil also known as Satan has sought always to steal, kill, and destroy anything that is of God on the earth. This includes the creation, subjects, and reign of God on the earth. He still seeks to compete with God and, with the help of the angels who fell with him (also known as fallen angels or evil spirits), he tries to rule over God's creation on the earth.

Who opposeth and exalteth himself above all that is called God, or that is worshipped; so that he as God sitteth in the temple of God, shewing himself that he is God.

2 Thessalonians 2:4

Hence Satan has his own kingdom known as the kingdom of darkness. This kingdom is at war with the Kingdom of God. It seeks to oppose and destroy anything that represents God's Kingdom, and to turn God's creation away from the worship, reflection, and service of God. It will use deceit, manipulation, seduction, pride, lust, and every evil method that it can fabricate to achieve its goal. We call this system of operation of Satan's kingdom "the world system". It is the present predominant system of operation in the earth today. It works contrary to God's Kingdom in operation. We also call it Babylon.

Our Purpose and Position in the Kingdom

Man was made by God to worship, reflect, and serve God.

Then saith Jesus unto him, Get thee hence, Satan: for it is written, Thou shalt worship the Lord thy God, and him only shalt thou serve.

Matthew 4:10

But ye are a chosen generation, a <u>royalpriesthood</u>, an holy nation, a peculiar people; that ye should <u>shew</u>*(display)* <u>forth the praises</u> *(virtues)*of him who hath called you out of darkness into his marvellous light;

1 Peter 2:9

It is from these three functions that we derive the ministries of man as a Priest, Son, and King.

"And have made us <u>kings</u> and <u>priests</u> to our God...."

Revelation 5:10

1. Man as Priest. The priestly ministry refers to our walk with God. It envisions us as priests unto God. The priestly ministry or office from the Old Testament through to the New Testament was seen as the office where men communed with God or represented the people to God. It was a noble office given only to the tribe of Levi. No other tribe was allowed to become a lineage of priests. Through salvation, every veil that stood in our way between God and man is removed and we have direct access to God (Hebrews 10:19-21). In this New Testament times, we who are all children of God become a royal priesthood unto God.

But ye are a chosen generation, a royal priesthood, an holy nation, a peculiar people; thatye should show forth the praises of him who hath called you out of darkness into his marvellous light:

1 Peter 2:9

We refer to our priestly ministry as our walk or fellowship with God. We also call it our vertical relationship. And this is our relationship with God as a friend. And just like the priest in the Old Testament it is the duty of the priests to offer sacrifices of worship unto God. It becomes our duty to worship God. Our priestly ministry involves prayer, study of the word, worship, giving, fasting, walking in righteousness, and obedience to God, etc.

It is from these acts of worship we gain access into the wisdom, power, character, and other strengths of God. Our priestly ministry therefore becomes the strength for our operation on the earth, since it is our daily act of fellowship with the Lord. It becomes the lifeline that empowers our operation in God's image and likeness on the earth. It acts like our fuel station where we refill ourselves with the life of God, so that we can keep manifesting like God on the earth in our Kingly Ministry.

2.Man as a Son. Our son-ship position as earlier taught under the chapter on "The new creation",is where as a new creature in Christ we have inherited the nature or genes of Christ Jesus, and have been restored back into the true image and likeness of God. We therefore as His ambassadors on the earth should radiate or reflect the person and glory of God on the earth.

Who being the brightness of his glory, and the express image of his person, and upholding all things by the word of his power, when he had by himself purged our sins, sat down on the right hand of the Majesty on high;

Hebrews 1:3

To whom God would make known what is the riches of the glory of this mystery among the Gentiles; which is Christ in you, the hope of glory:

Colossians 1:27

Herein is our love made perfect, that we may have boldness in the day of judgment: because as he is, so are we in this world.

1 John 4:17

We become God's reflection in this world and a shining light that radiates His reality on the earth today.

Ye are the light of the world. A city that is set on an hill cannot be hid.
Neither do men light a candle, and put it under a bushel, but on a candlestick; and it giveth light unto all that are in the house.
Let your light so shine before men, that they may see your good works, and glorify your Father which is in heaven.

Matthew 5:14-16

3. Man as King. Our kingly ministry has to do with our service unto God. God made the earth as an extension of His Kingdom. Adam was to have dominion and rule on behalf of God over the earth. The earth belongs to God, but He gave it to men. Yet Adam handed it to Satan the minute he disobeyed God in the Garden of Eden (rejecting God as his Master) and obeyed Satan by eating the fruit (enthroning Satan as his new ruler). Hence Satan and his kingdom began to rule over the inhabitants of the earth. This was not God's original plan or will. God seeks to re-establish His Kingdom once again over the whole earth and its inhabitants.

For the LORD most high is terrible; he is a great King over all the earth.
He shall subdue the people under us, and the nations under our feet.

Psalm 47:2-3

Thy kingdom come. Thy will be done in earth, as it is in heaven.

Matthew 6:10

In order for God to rule over this earth he must use His citizens on the earth to establish His Kingdom and will on the earth. These are the children of God who are subject to God and His will. All of us who are now in Christ have been redeemed by the blood of Jesus and remain in the earth so that we can finish the work or business of our heavenly Father in reconciling the earth back to Himself.

And all things are of God, who hath reconciled us to himself by Jesus Christ, and hathgiven to us the ministry of reconciliation;

To wit, that God was in Christ, reconciling the world unto himself, not imputing their trespasses unto them; and hath committed unto us the word of reconciliation.

2 Corinthians 5:18-19

This is the assignment given to all children of God on the earth. We are to reconcile (bring back into perfect harmony and submission) all the inhabitants, geography, resources, and social systems of the world to God. We are to restore the dominion of God's Kingdom over the earth and its inhabitants. We are to bring forth into the earth and administrate the Kingdom of God on the earth. This assignment therefore makes us kings or governors of God's Kingdom on the earth.

We are to serve God in our unique areas of calling and purpose in life. It is specifically narrowed down to our God ordained purposes in life. Every person has his/her own area of calling which God has given to them to represent Christ and reign on His behalf. The kingly ministry therefore seeks to infiltrate God's Kingdom into every of the professional, geographical, and language based worlds through our services and expertise that is in line with our God ordained purpose.

We are kings subject to the King of kings (Christ Jesus). And we are kings who are appointed not to oppress the people but to serve the people into God's reign, purposes, will, righteousness, and excellence.

TEST YOURSELF
CHAPTER 2 – THE KINGDOM OF GOD

The answer sheet is provided at the back of this manual.

1. What does the word the "Kingdom of God" refer to:

   a) This is the region, territory, people, geography, resources, and civilization that are under the rule, reign, or influence of God as their King.
   b) A place in space where the angels live.
   c) Ability to please God in what we do.
   d) The nation of Israel and its tribes.

2. Which one of this sentence best defines Our Kingly ministry:

   a) Our Love unto our Lord.
   b) Our Service unto the Lord.
   c) Our sacrifices unto the Lord.
   d) Our Praising unto the Lord.

3. Which one of the following best describes man's purpose on earth:

   a) To buy a Mercedes and become successful.
   b) To climb up to the top of his/her career ladder.
   c) To worship, reflect, and serve God.
   d) To become good church members.

4. The kingdom of darkness in its operations can also be referred to as the

   _____.

5. The fulfilment of man's purpose would have him/her function as a priest, a son, and_____.

CHAPTER 3:

RIGHTEOUSNESS

A righteous God and a Kingdom of righteousness

Because God is Righteous (Psalm 129:4 & Psalm 145:17) and one of His names is God our Righteousness (Jeremiah 23:6), the Kingdom of God is a Kingdom of righteousness (Romans 14:17). The Kingdom takes on the nature of its king.

In his days Judah shall be saved, and Israel shall dwell safely: and this is his name whereby he shall be called, THE LORD OUR RIGHTEOUSNESS.

Jeremiah 23:6

For the kingdom of God is not meat and drink; but righteousness, and peace, and joy in the Holy Ghost.

Romans 14:17

Therefore, wherever the righteousness of God is, the Kingdom of God comes into manifestation.

The Lord reigneth; let the earth rejoice; let the multitude of isles be glad thereof. Clouds and darkness are round about him: righteousness and judgment are the habitation of his throne.

Psalm 97:1-2

God executes and administrates His Kingdom according to His righteousness. Therefore good understanding of God's righteousness is important in order to properly access, enforce, administrate, enjoy, and propagate the Kingdom of God in one's life and over the earth.

Definition of righteousness

The words 'righteousness' and 'righteous' in God's Kingdom mean more than just walking in holiness, or even having right standing with God. In the Old and New Testament scriptures it is translated from certain Hebrew and Greek words used in the original writing of these books, which when carefully examined help give us a better understanding of the words 'righteous' and 'righteousness'.
Putting the meanings of all these words together, both from the Hebrew and the Greek words, and using the context within which these words are used in scripture, we derive deeper meanings according to God's Kingdom.

Righteousness in God's Kingdom can therefore be defined as:

1. Righteous nature and Right standing with God. After accepting Jesus Christ as Lord and Saviour, the new born believer receives the Life of God which enables his/her spirit man to both be reborn into God's own true image and to inherit God's righteous nature. He/she by reason of this nature becomes the righteousness of God in Christ and is no longer a sinner by nature. This new inherited nature of God's righteousness by which the believer is now clothed acquires for the born again believer in Christ right standing (relationship and acceptance) with God.

Therefore if any man be in Christ, he is a new creature: old things are passed away; behold, all things are become new.
For he hath made him to be sin for us, who knew no sin; that we might be made the righteousness of God in him.

2 Corinthians 5:17 & :21

2. Having a right heart. This means our priorities, desires, motives, beliefs, and our attitudes should be right.

Thou hast neither part nor lot in this matter: for thy heart is not right in the sight of God.

Acts 8:21

3. Right thinking. We are to think right, in line and in harmony with the thoughts of God. This is called the mind of Christ.

Finally, brethren, whatsoever things are true, whatsoever things are honest, whatsoever things are just, whatsoever things are pure, whatsoever things are lovely, whatsoever things are of good report; if there be any virtue, and if there be any praise, think on these things.

Philippians 4:8

4. Making right decisions and choices (judgement). We as God's children should make our judgement (decision making) according to and in harmony with His righteousness.

Simon answered and said, I suppose that he, to whom he forgave most. And he said unto him, Thou hast rightly judged.

Luke 7:43

5. Administering justice and equity. We as God's children should be just and equitable towards others at all times.

But with righteousness shall he judge the poor, and reprove with equity for the meek of the earth: and he shall smite the earth: with the rod of his mouth, and with the breath of his lips shall he slay the wicked.

Isaiah 11:4

6. Right speaking. We should speak right words at all times. Speaking in harmony with God's will and words for every situation.

I have not spoken in secret, in a dark place of the earth: I said not unto the seed of Jacob, Seek ye me in vain: I the Lord <u>speak righteousness</u>, I declare things that are right.

Isaiah 45:19

Death and life are in the power of the tongue: and they that love it shall eat the fruit thereof.

Proverbs 18:21

7. Right living (holiness). Holiness is a part of righteousness, just like football is a part of sports, but not all of sports. Holiness is being separated and dedicated unto God. Separated from the world and the evil lifestyle that is in it and keeping oneself from the works of the flesh.

Love not the world, neither the things that are in the world. If any man love the world, the love of the Father is not in him.
For all that is in the world, the lust of the flesh, and the lust of the eyes, and the pride of life, is not of the Father, but is of the world.

1 John 2:15-16

8. Doing right. This has to do with doing the right thing or carrying out the right action that would produce the right result. Just like Jesus did the right thing (lawful) in healing the man with the withered hand on the Sabbath day.

And, behold, there was a man which had his hand withered. And they asked him, saying, <u>Is it lawful to heal on the Sabbath days?</u>that they might accuse him.
And he said unto them, What man shall there be among you, that shall have one sheep, and if it fall into a pit on the sabbath day, will he not lay hold on it, and lift it out?
How much then is a man better than a sheep? Wherefore it is lawful to do well on the sabbath days.
Then saith he to the man, Stretch forth thine hand. And he stretched it forth; and it was restored whole, like as the other.

Matthew 12:10-13

9. Acting in line with God's purposes and will. Our righteous nature should cause us to live in line with Gods purpose and will for us, submitting to God's will and purposes.

Jesus saith unto them, My meat is to do the will of him that sent me, and to finish his work.

John 4:34

10. You have rights as a citizen of God's Kingdom. This means that as a citizen of God's kingdom, the strengths and benefits of the Kingdom are your inheritance by right. Salvation is not something you beg for as a son of God, but it is your right.

The righteous shall inherit the land, and dwell therein for ever.

Psalm 37:29

11. The Kingdom of God has rights over you. As a citizen of God's Kingdom, you belong to God and the Kingdom, and you are to be subject to the laws of that Kingdom.

For he that is called in the Lord, being a servant, is the Lord's freeman: likewise also he that is called, being free, is Christ's servant.

1 Corinthians 7:22

12. Walking in Divine Order.

Let all things be done decently and in order.

1 Corinthians 14:40

God is a God of order. His Kingdom has an order of doing things, which is very contrary to the world's order. God's Kingdom order is referred to as divine order. God's order is in harmony with His word. The principles that govern God's Kingdom constitute the order of His Kingdom.

Divine order needs to be put into place wherever people want to experience the governance of God. God works with you when you put His order into place in your situation (Mark 16:20). We should put this order in place in our personal lives, our families, Church, business and professional life, communities, nations, and any other relationship where we seek to enjoy and experience the Kingdom of God in manifestation.

Righteousness means all these combined, which in turn gives it a deeper, and yet more practical meaning.

TEST YOURSELF
CHAPTER 3 – RIGHTEOUSNESS

The answer sheet is provided at the back of this manual.

1. Which of the following does not define righteousness?

   a) Right thinking.
   b) Eating with a fork and a knife.
   c) Having a right heart.
   d) Walking in divine order.

2. Which of the following statements is not true about righteousness?

   a) God executes and administrates His Kingdom according to His righteousness.
   b) Wherever the righteousness of God is, the Kingdom of God comes into manifestation.
   c) God is Righteous and one of His names is God our Righteousness.
   d) Righteousness is our own high standards of obeying God.

3. What is the definition of Holiness?

   a) Separated from the world and the evil lifestyle that is in it and keeping oneself from the works of the flesh.
   b) Attending church every Sunday and taking notes.
   c) Singing Holy songs from the Hymn book.
   d) Reading my Bible every day.

4. The word _____ in God's Kingdom means more than just walking in holiness, or even having right standing with God.

5. As a Citizen of God's Kingdom, you belong to God and to_____, and you are to be subject to the laws of that Kingdom.

CHAPTER 4:

SALVATION

What is salvation?

Salvation is a prominent theme in the body of Christ. However it connotes different meanings to different people. To some it connotes the forgiveness of sin only, to others a ticket to heaven, to others deliverance from the troubles of this life, and on and on.

Neither is there salvation in any other: for there is none other name under heaven given among men, whereby we must be saved.
                                                                                    Acts 4:12

For I am not ashamed of the gospel of Christ: for it is the power of God unto salvation to everyone that believeth; to the Jew first, and also to the Greek.
                                                                                    Romans 1:16

But what truly does salvation entail? This is important because without a proper understanding of the same, we are limited in terms of what we understand it to mean. The word salvation is from the Greek word **"soteria"** which means total wellness of being. The wellness of being here makes reference to every area of life i.e. spirit, soul, and body according to 1 Thessalonians 5:23. Soteriaentails being born again, deliverance, safety, health, prosperity (in every area of one's social life), protection, posterity, and soundness of mind.

Let us consider the following scriptures to aid our understanding.

But he was wounded for our transgressions, he was bruised for our iniquities: thechastisement of our peace was upon him; and with his stripes we are healed.
                                                                                    Isaiah 53:5

I am come that they might have life, and that they might have it more abundantly.
                                                                                    John 10:10

Jesus did not only die to take away our sins but he also suffered for our peace (wellness and wholeness of being, spiritually, soulically, and physically). Jesus died so you could have and enjoy Life (Zoe). The life Jesus was talking about was the God kind of life called Zoe. This is God's kind of life that produces in/for us safety, deliverance, success, long life, health etc. This is living the God kind of life on the earth. This is what He came to give not just forgiveness of sin or healing from sickness.

For God so loved the world, that he gave his only begotten Son, that whosoever believeth in him should not perish, but have everlasting life*(Zoe)*.

John 3:16

Many Christians know that they have received salvation through Jesus Christ, but they do not understand fully what salvation means. As a result they confine themselves to a few of the benefits of salvation while they tolerate the absence of healing, prosperity, safety, soundness of mind, etc.

Bless the LORD, O my soul, and forget not all his benefits:
Who forgiveth all thine iniquities; who healeth all thy diseases;
Who redeemeth thy life from destruction; who crowneth thee with lovingkindness and tender mercies;
Who satisfieth thy mouth with good things; so that thy youth is renewed like theeagle's.
The LORD executeth righteousness and judgment for all that are oppressed.

Psalm 103:2-6

We should not forget these benefits of salvation which Jesus Christ our Lord and Saviour suffered and died to secure for us as in Isaiah 53:5. We should be ever mindful and conscious of it. It is yours today. Jesus has paid the price for us all. It does not need to be paid for again. It is your right as a child of God.

Working out your salvation

(For he saith, I have heard thee in a time accepted, and in the day of salvation have I succoured thee: behold, now is the accepted time; behold, now is the day of salvation.)

2 Corinthians 6:2

The salvation package is to be enjoyed now. Jesus died more than two thousand years ago to secure it for us. It is available to us at every given point in time. The reason why many believers are not able to access salvation is primarily due to both ignorance and the lack of diligence to work it out.

1. Ignorance. Ignorance is one of the greatest enemies of the people of God. This is because it blinds our mind from seeing what our inheritance, rights and privileges are in Christ. It also blinds us from knowing what needs to be done to wisely activate our salvation into reality on the earth.

My people are destroyed for lack of knowledge: because thou hast rejected knowledge, I will also reject thee, that thou shalt be no priest to me: seeing thou hast forgotten the law of thy God, I will also forget thy children.
As they were increased, so they sinned against me: therefore will I change theirglory into shame.

Hosea 4:6-7

God Himself attributes the destruction and shame (loss of God's glory) of His covenant people to ignorance. This is ignorance of the word of God, which teaches us the ways of God. Therefore, when we are ignorant of God's Word we are ignorant of God's ways. This was the difference between Moses and the Israelites (Psalm 103:7), Moses knew God's ways, while the Israelites didn't. It is the truths in God's word which when we apply that sets us free.

Then said Jesus to those Jews which believed on him, If ye continue in my word, then are ye my disciples indeed;
And ye shall know the truth, and the truth shall make you free.

John 6:31-32

Paul in writing to Timothy wrote of how Timothy through the knowledge of the scriptures had learnt how to wisely access his salvation package in Christ Jesus.

And that from a child thou hast known the holy scriptures, which are able to make thee wise unto salvation through faith which is in Christ Jesus.

2 Timothy 3:15

2. Diligently work at it. The scriptures show us the promises of God towards us in every area of salvation (soteria). They also show us what to do to access our salvation. There is always a condition in the scriptures assigned to every promise of God.

The word of God is like a seed. It needs to be planted in order for it to bring forth fruit (results). Acting on and speaking God's word is like planting a seed. It is only after we have fulfilled the relevant conditions assigned to a given promise of salvation in the scripture that we can and should expect tangible results. It is through our speech and actions that we activate our salvation, which Jesus Christ secured for us all.

Be not deceived; God is not mocked: for whatsoever a man soweth, that shall he also reap.

Galatians 6:7

Acting wisely on God's word is acting in faith. This is because we act on it expecting God to work with us (as in division of labour) to give the increase and desired results.

And they went forth, and preached everywhere, the Lord working with them, andconfirming the word with signs following. Amen.

Mark 16:20

Hence, our duty is to rightly apply the word of God in faith through our speech and action. This way the word of God becomes our lifestyle. We shall learn more on how to study and act on the word of God in the chapter on the word of God.

Salvation is our inheritance through Christ Jesus, yet we also have a role to play in birthing it into the earth. While it is part of the finished works of Jesus Christ, yet He needs our wise cooperation in order for it to become a reality in our lives. We are responsible to initiate it in the earth. We therefore need to be diligent (careful and hardworking) in order for us to experience our salvation. We are commanded in the scriptures to work it out. This we do by wisely and diligently applying God's word with patience to our situation.

Wherefore, my beloved, as ye have always obeyed, not as in my presence only, but now much more in my absence, work out your own salvation with fear and trembling.

Philippians 2:12

This involves our participation, hence the term working it out.

TEST YOURSELF:
CHAPTER 4 – SALVATION

The answer sheet is provided at the back of this manual.

1. Which Greek word carries the true meaning of the English word "salvation"?

   a) Soteria
   b) Christ
   c) Peace
   d) Prosperity

2. The God kind of life is also referred to as?

   a) Zoe
   b) Health
   c) Prosperity
   d) Salvation

3. When we are ignorant of God's word, we are ignorant of?

   a) God's ways
   b) Good ideas
   c) Our pastors
   d) Good things

4. Salvation makes reference to

   _____ in

   every area of life (spirit, soul, and body).

5. One of the major reasons why many believers are not able to enjoy the fullness of
   Salvation is because of _____

   _____.

CHAPTER 5:

THE JOURNEY TO SALVATION

Man in God's image and likeness

And God said, Let us make man in our image, after our likeness: and let them have dominion over the fish of the sea, and over the fowl of the air, and over thecattle, and over all the earth, and over every creeping thing that creepeth upon the earth.
So God created man in his own image, in the image of God created he him; male and female created he them.

Genesis 1:26-27

God being a spirit (John 4:24) means man was also made a spirit. Yet this spirit called man, lives in a physical body. Man being in God's image meant man looks like God and is like God in being. When we say something is an image of an object we are talking of it being a replica to some certain dimension of that object. Just like an Elephant would birth a baby elephant that will grow up to be like the adult elephant, so it is with God and man. God birthed (Genesis 2:7) a man in His image who would grow to function like God on the earth. This man belongs to God's family just like the baby elephant belongs to the elephant family.

As a result of being in the image of God this man would also be able to function like God in the earth. He can do on the earth what God does in the heavens. Likeness talks of abilities of operation. Meaning man could function or operate like God. He can laugh, talk and walk like God. He can rule and have dominion over all creation and creatures on the earth like God. He can rule over and rectify every situation like God did in Genesis 1:3. Man was like a little god on the earth. Not to be worshiped but to administrate the earth for God. Man was to rule over the earth and God's creation on the earth. He was to represent God as God's ambassador on the earth. The earth was to be an extension of God's Kingdom. Adam was the administrator of God's Kingdom on the earth.

The fall of man

And the LORD God commanded the man, saying, Of every tree of the garden thou mayest freely eat:

But of the tree of the knowledge of good and evil, thou shalt not eat of it: for in the day that thou eatest thereof thou shalt surely die.

Genesis 2:16-17

God gave a command to man and the consequence of disobeying God was death. This death was not just physical death only, because we know from the scriptures that the day Adam and Eve ate of the fruit of knowledge of good and evil they still continued to exist on the earth. This death was a spiritual death as a result of the loss of the life of God (known as Zoe) within man. Man was a spirit being full of the very Life of God known as Zoe. The day man ate of the fruit God had commanded him not to eat, he (man) lost that Life of God called Zoe. This Zoe is also called everlasting life (Matthew 19:29) or eternal life (Matthew 19:16) in scripture.

We shall consider five major things that happened as a result of this loss of life (Zoe). They are:

1. Man lost the nature and glory of God. When man lost the life of God, he also lost his true nature which was the nature of God, he was transformed into another creature (a fallen creature called fallen adamic man) other than what God made man to be, and he inherited and put on the nature of the devil which was one of sin and death.

For all have sinned, and come short of the glory of God;

Romans 3:23

As a result of this loss of life, man fell short of the glory (image and likeness) of God. This meant man lost God's life and divine nature. This Zoe was what made man (the spirit part of man) of the very stuff and matter of God.

2. Physical death came into the earth and creation. As a result of spiritual death physical death ate in slowly, and this death also permeated into every area of man's life and social existence. This was a consequence of man's wrong choice which God had enlightened man of in Genesis 3:15-19. All of creation began to undergo corruption due to death.

For the creature was made subject to vanity, not willingly, but by reason of him who hath subjected the same in hope,
For we know that the whole creation groaneth and travaileth in pain together untilnow.

Romans 8:20& 22

3. Man was alienated from true fellowship with God. Man also became spiritually alienated from God as a result of this loss of Zoe (Ephesians 4:17-19). He no longer belonged to the family of God just like a snake does not belong to the family of a lion. God had to set boundaries in His relationship with man due to the loss of man's original nature (God's nature) and positioning of relationship with God.

So he drove out the man; and he placed at the east of the garden of Eden Cherubims, and a flaming sword which turned every way, to keep the way of the tree of life.

Genesis 3:24

God could not relate in His original intended way to this fallen man who was no more operating at God's frequency. This can be likened to how a man cannot relate and fellowship satisfactorily with an ant. The ant is a lesser creature who cannot communicate on man's level of fellowship and communication.

4. Man could not spend eternity with God. Heaven would never allow sin to walk through its gates. God rejects and detests sin. The sinful nature of man is as a result of the loss of the life of God in man. Man as a spirit being became a sinner, not because of how he lives, but because his nature was now that of a sinner. All his descendants were born with this same sinful nature as every creature brings forth according to its kind (Romans 3:23).

Jesus answered, Verily, verily, I say unto thee, Except a man be born of water and of the Spirit, he cannot enter into the kingdom of God.
And no man hath ascended up to heaven, but he that came down from heaven, even theSon of man which is in heaven.

John 3:5 & 13

As a result no man could enter into heaven unless their nature was changed from sin. How we live our lives cannot change our sin nature. All men who walked with God before Jesus died had to go to a waiting paradise until Jesus came to pay for their redemption. Luke 16:22 and 1 Peter 4:6.

5. Man was hell bound. When man sinned he sentenced himself to eternity in the place of the wicked. This is the lake of fire, a place prepared for the devil and his fallen angels (Matthew 25:41). Hell with all its occupants would also eventually be cast into the lake of fire along with death and Satan (Revelation 20:10&14-15). Man was destined to hell and the lake of fire to pay the full punishment for sin, which is eternal death.

For the wages of sin is death;………

Romans 6:23

The remedy

For God so loved the world, that he gave his only begotten Son, that whosoever believeth in him should not perish, but have everlasting life.
For God sent not his Son into the world to condemn the world; but that the world through him might be saved.

John 3:16-17

I am come that they might have life, and that they might have it more abundantly.

John 10:10

God's love for man would not allow Him to leave man in the state man was in. God already had a way of escape for man. The solution was to restore the life of God (Zoe) back to man thereby restoring mankind back into oneness and family with God.

As thou hast given him power over all flesh, that he should give eternal life to as many as thou hast given him.
And this is life eternal, that they might know thee the only true God, and Jesus Christ, whom thou hast sent.

John 17:2-3

God by sending Jesus Christ to die for man restored back the life of God (Zoe) to man. This restored man back into God's image and likeness, and back into oneness of fellowship with God. This reconciliation allows man to spend eternity with God, and to avoid paying for his sins or spending eternity tormented in the lake of fire.

The Lamb of God

Jesus became the ultimate sacrifice for our sins. Someone had to pay the full price for the sins and fall of man. The price was death as seen in Genesis 2:17. Man had to die for his sin and spend eternity in the lake of fire alienated from God. But not anymore, because Jesus Christ became our substitute by dying in our place.He lovingly gave Himself to pay for man's eternal crime so that mankind would not have to pay for it again.

But God commendeth his love toward us, in that, while we were yet sinners, Christ died for us.
Much more then, being now justified by his blood, we shall be saved from wrath through him.
For if, when we were enemies, we were reconciled to God by the death of his Son, much more, being reconciled, we shall be saved by his life.
And not only so, but we also joy in God through our Lord Jesus Christ, by whom we have now received the atonement.

Romans 5:8-11

He not only took all the sin of mankind, but also went to the place where all wicked men were doomed to go (hell) and thereby paid the full punishment for our sentence. You and I do not have to pay it any more. We do not have to go to hell.

But he was wounded for our transgressions, he was bruised for our iniquities: thechastisement of our peace was upon him; and with his stripes we are healed.
All we like sheep have gone astray; we have turned everyone to his own way; and the LORD hath laid on him the iniquity of us all.
He was oppressed, and he was afflicted, yet he opened not his mouth: he is brought as a lamb to the slaughter, and as a sheep before her shearers is dumb, so he openeth not his mouth.
He was taken from prison and from judgment: and who shall declare his generation? For he was cut off out of the land of the living: for the transgression of my people was he stricken.
And <u>he made his grave with the wicked</u>, and with the rich in his death; because

he had done no violence, neither was any deceit in his mouth.
Yet it pleased the LORD to bruise him; he hath put him to grief: when thou shalt make his soul an offering for sin, he shall see his seed, he shall prolong his days, and the pleasure of the LORD shall prosper in his hand.

Isaiah 53:5-10

Our High Priest

He became our High Priest by opening up for us a new line of fellowship with God. Through Jesus we now have access to fellowship with the Godhead. There is no other way to access fellowship with God but through Jesus.

Jesus saith unto him, I am the way, the truth, and the life: no man cometh unto the Father, but by me.

John 14:6

No other religion washes away and changes our sin nature inherited from the devil through the fall of man. No other religion pays the price of going to hell for the sins of man. No other religion truly reconciles mankind back to proper fellowship with God.

And their sins and iniquities will I remember no more.
Now where remission ofthese is, there is no more offering for sin.
Having therefore, brethren, boldness to enter into the holiest by the blood of Jesus,
By a new and living way, which hehath consecrated for us, through the veil, that is to say, his flesh;
And having anhigh priest over the house of God;
Let us draw near with a true heart in full assurance of faith, having our hearts
Sprinkled from an evil conscience, and our bodies washed with pure water.

Hebrews 10:17-22

As our priest He becomes our bridge to God, the only mediator between God and man. Through Him we have access to the Father and vice versa. Even in our short comings, Christ our High Priest stands in the gap for us with the Father. He knows what we go through and is therefore well placed to be our mediator (Hebrew 4:16).

As our priest, He receives our sacrifices of praise, prayer, worship, giving etc. He aids us, as the priests in the Old Testament did to connect the people with God. He strengthens us in the counsel of God.

King of Kings

We all become children of God (members of God's family) as a result of the Life (Zoe) and nature of God that is restored to us. We also become citizens of God's Kingdom and are once more restored into God's image and likeness.

This means we are to function like God on the earth and administrate God's Kingdom on the earth (Luke 2:49). We are to rule like Kings (or governors) of God's Kingdom on the earth, and over our various areas of calling. Yet, Jesus Christ remains the King of this Kingdom and the head of the Church, hence making Him the King of all Kings of this kingdom.

And they sing the song of Moses the servant of God, and the song of the Lamb,saying, Great and marvellous are thy works, Lord God Almighty; just and true arethy ways, thou King of saints.

Revelations 15:3

These shall make war with the Lamb, and the Lamb shall overcome them: for heis Lord of lords, and King of kings: and they that are with him are called, andchosen, and faithful.

Revelations 17:14

Just as every King has a kingdom within which He rules, Jesus becomes our new ruler. We live by His decree and statutes. We are subject to Him. He is now seated on the throne of our lives. He brings us into a lineage of Kings unto Him and we partake of His royalty (1 Peter 2:9). We now seek to spread His Kingdom to the ends of the earth (Isaiah 9:7).

The way to salvation

This is done by acknowledging and accepting the finished work of salvation that Christ worked for us. There is only one way of receiving the life (Zoe) of God. This is by accepting Jesus Christ as one's personal Lord and Saviour (John 14:6).

That if thou shalt confess with thy mouth the Lord Jesus, and shalt believe in thine heart that God hath raised him from the dead, thou shalt be saved.
For with the heart man believeth unto righteousness; and with the mouth confession is made unto salvation.
For whosoever shall call upon the name of the Lord shall be saved.

Romans 10:9-10 & 13

The scriptures show that whosoever shall confess Jesus Christ (either in prayer or speech) as his/her Lord and Saviour, believing in their heart that Christ died for their redemption, and that He is raised from the dead, shall be saved.

This means that the Life of God would be restored into that individual by the Holy Ghost, and that individual's spirit would instantly be changed back (hence the term born again) into a new creature in the nature and image of God. Such a person has within themselves the potential to once again walk in the likeness of God.

Jesus answered and said unto him, Verily, verily, I say unto thee, Except a man be born again, he cannot see the kingdom of God.

Nicodemus saith unto him, How can a man be born when he is old? can he enter the second time into his mother's womb, and be born?
Jesus answered, Verily, verily, I say unto thee, Except a man be born of water andof the Spirit, he cannot enter into the kingdom of God.
That which is born of the flesh is flesh; and that which is born of the Spirit is spirit.

John 3:3-6

Therefore if any man be in Christ, he is a new creature: old things are passed away; behold, all things are become new.

2 Corinthians 5:17

TEST YOURSELF:
CHAPTER 5 – THE JOURNEY TO SALVATION

The answer sheet is provided at the back of this manual.

1. Can a person who dies as a Buddhist go to heaven?

   a) Yes, if he/she does a lot of good works.
   b) Yes, if he/she seeks forgiveness from all he/she has ever wronged.
   c) Yes, if he contributes regularly to charity.
   d) No.

2. If wicked, unrighteous, and evil man believes in the sacrifice Jesus Christ paid for him by His death and resurrection, and declares sincerely with his mouth to a friend that Jesus is his Lord and Saviour, would he become born-again?

   a) Yes.
   b) No.
   c) Maybe.
   d) Not immediately.

3. Which one of the following does not represent the consequences of man's falling away through sin:

   a) He lost the nature and glory of God.
   b) He brought physical death into the earth and creation.
   c) He was connected to true fellowship with God.
   d) He was disconnected from spending eternity with God.

4. When Adam disobeyed God in the garden he lost the _____ of God also known as "Zoe" in the Greek language.

5. God through Jesus Christ's death and resurrection restored man back into God's image and likeness and back into _____ of fellowship with God.

CHAPTER 6:

THE DYNAMICS OF MAN

Man as a triune being

And the very God of peace sanctify you wholly; and I pray God your whole <u>spirit</u> and <u>soul</u> and <u>body</u> be preserved blameless unto the coming of our Lord Jesus Christ.

1 Thessalonians 5:23

The above scripture talks of God sanctifying man wholly. This means every part of man. It goes on to talk of the sanctifying of man's **spirit** and **soul** and **body**. By making reference to the whole of man, we see the three parts of man or the triune nature of man.

From this information we can deduce that man is a spirit, who lives inside a physical body, and possesses a soul. We shall look at each aspect of man more closely in other studies. A good illustration is that of an Astronaut in space who has to put on a space suit in order to dwell on the moon, and communicates and expresses himself through a communication radio. The Astronaut is the spirit being, the space suit is the human body, and the communication gadget is the soul of man.

Man is a spirit being

God is a Spirit being (John 4:24) and He made man in His own image and after His likeness, it therefore means that man was also made a spirit being (Genesis 1:26). This is why when a person dies he still lives on beyond this earth. Man exists as a spirit being.

And <u>her spirit</u> came again, and she arose straightway: and he commanded to giveher meat.

Luke 8:55

And the child grew, and waxed strong <u>in spirit</u>, filled with wisdom: and the graceof God was upon him.

Luke 2:40

And it came to pass in the morning that <u>his spirit</u> was troubled; and he sent andcalled for all the magicians of Egypt, and all the wise men thereof: and

Pharaohtold them his dream; but there was none that could interpret them unto Pharaoh.

Genesis 41:8

The Hebrew word used for "spirit" is the same word used for the "breath" that God breathed into the physical body of man. God breathed spirit into the body formed from the ground, and this brought life into the body, causing the soul of the man to come alive.

And the Lord God formed man of the dust of the ground, and breathed into his nostrils the <u>breath</u> of life; and man became a living soul.

Genesis 2:7

Man's spirit is the centre of his being. It is his connection with God. Through it man develops God consciousness and is in touch with the spirit world or spiritual realities.

But let it be <u>the hidden man of the heart</u>, in that which is not corruptible, even the ornament of a meek and quiet spirit, which is in the sight of God of great price.

1 Peter 3:4

Keep thy heart with all diligence; for out of it are the issues of life.

Proverbs 4:23

The <u>spirit of man</u> is the candle of the Lord, searching all the inward parts of the belly.

Proverbs 20:27

It was man as a spirit being that inherited the sinful nature of the devil when Adam sinned in the Garden of Eden and lost the life and nature of God. Man still existed as a spirit being but was now alienated from God due to the absence of God's life and nature. He was no longer a member of God's family or kind. The spirit man became another creature other than what God made it to be, and a lesser being called fallen man.

This I say therefore, and testify in the Lord, that ye henceforth walk not as other Gentiles walk, in the vanity of their mind,
Having the understanding darkened, <u>being alienated from the life of God</u> through the ignorance that is in them, because of the blindness of their heart:

Ephesians 4:17-18

But now that Jesus Christ has opened for us a new way of reconciliation with God, whoever receives salvation inherits the life of God and the spirit being is instantly reborn into the exact image and likeness of God. The person (as a spirit) becomes a new creature. Man's spirit is restored back to God. Man can now know and fellowship with God on a greater level of intimacy. He now has potential for a closer level of intimacy and walk with God because God now dwells on his inside. He has become the dwelling place and the temple of God.

Know ye not that ye are the temple of God, and that the Spirit of God dwellethinyou?

1 Corinthians 3:16

Be ye not unequally yoked together with unbelievers: for what fellowship hath righteousness with unrighteousness? and what communion hath light with darkness?
And what concord hath Christ with Belial? or what part hath he that believeth with an infidel?
And what agreement hath the temple of God with idols? for ye are the temple of the living God; as God hath said, I will dwell in them, and walk in them; and I will be their God, and they shall be my people.

2 Corinthians 6:14-16

The human soul

Man is a spirit being who possesses a soul. The soul of man is not the same as the spirit of a man. The scriptures say that the word of God can divide between the spirit and the soul of a man.

For the word of God is quick, and powerful, and sharper than any twoedged sword, <u>piercing even to the dividing asunder of soul and spirit,</u> and of the joints and marrow, and is a discerner of the thoughts and intents of the heart.

Hebrews 4:12

The soul of man consists of his will (for making choices), his mind (comprising his intellect, imagination, and memory) and his emotions (comprising his affections, desires, and senses). They become man's expressive channel through which he/she communicates with the outside world or expresses himself. The soul is therefore the self-conscious part of man, through which he stays in touch with himself and the outside world. It is also the connection between his/her spirit and body.

The soul of man does not get born again instantly during the salvation of the spirit of man. It goes through a life process of continuous restoration or salvation into the soul/mind of God. The life of God begins to flood the mind, emotions, and will of man, making them to function or operate on the frequency of God.

Receiving the end of your faith, <u>even the salvation of your souls</u>.
Seeing ye have purified your souls in obeying the truth through the spirit unto unfeigned love of the brethren, see that ye love one another with a pure heart fervently:

1 Peter 1:9 & 22

Wherefore lay apart all filthiness and superfluity of naughtiness, and receive withmeekness the engrafted word, which is able to save your souls.

James 1:21

For who hath known the mind of the Lord, that he may instruct him? But we have the mind of Christ.

1 Corinthians 2:16

The saving of the soul under goes the following processes:

1. Taming the emotions. We learn to tame our emotions (killing the negative ungodly ones), bringing them to the service and aiding of God's purposes.

And they that are Christ's have crucified the flesh with the affections and lusts.

Galatians 5:24

2. Submitting our will. We learn to submit our will to God by choosing to walk in obedience to God's word, instructions, and will.

And he said, Abba, Father, all things are possible unto thee; take away this cup from me: nevertheless not what I will, but what thou wilt.

Mark 14:36

Furthermore we have had fathers of our flesh which corrected us, and we gave them reverence: shall we not much rather <u>be in subjection unto the Father of spirits</u>, and live?

Hebrews 12:9

3. Renewing our mind. We learn and begin to renew our mind and all its capability by studying the word of God, digging out and acting on the principles of God's Kingdom and the ways of God which we discover in God's word. It brings enlightenment of God's will, purposes, and righteousness to our mind, bringing our mind into harmony at all seasons with God's mind.

And be not conformed to this world: but be ye transformed by the renewing of your mind, that ye may prove what is that good, and acceptable, and perfect, will of God.

Romans 12:2

The human body

Man is a spirit being, who possesses a soul, and lives in a physical body. His body is not the person. It is the casing through which man gets legal ground to operate on the earth. His body provides residence for his spirit. It is like the space suit that the

Astronaut wears to stay in space. The human body is the earth suit or earthly tabernacle of man.

Yea, I think it meet, as long as <u>I am in this tabernacle</u>, to stir you up by putting you in remembrance;
Knowing that shortly <u>I must put off this my tabernacle</u>, even as our Lord Jesus Christ hath showed me.
Moreover I will endeavour that ye may be able after my decease to have these things always in remembrance

2 Peter 1:13-15

God made the human body (sometimes called the mortal body) from the dust of the ground. Then God breathed the human spirit into the body, and man's soul came alive or into operation. This made man a living soul.

And the LORD God formed man of the dust of the ground, and breathed into his nostrils the breath of life; and man became a living soul.

Genesis 2:7

It is not the same as the spirit of man as seen in Hebrews 4:12 and the scripture below.

Watch and pray, that ye enter not into temptation: <u>the spirit</u> indeed is willing, but the flesh is weak.

Matthew 26:41

Our bodies, which comprises of our genes/DNA, cells, organs, skeletal structure, members, systems, etc, also gradually partake of the life of God as the Holy Spirit works to quicken (give life to) our mortal or human bodies.

But if the Spirit of him that raised up Jesus from the dead dwell in you, he that raised up Christ from the dead shall also quicken your mortal bodies by his Spirit that dwelleth in you.

Romans 8:11

The effects of this new life upon our body supernaturally empowers it to overcome obstacles that would hinder us from fulfilling God's will e.g. death, disease, harm etc. This way our human body can be strong and healthy and serve us enough time on the earth to do and finish God's purposes and will.

According as his divine power hath given unto us all things that pertain unto life and godliness, through the knowledge of him that hath called us to glory and virtue:
Whereby are given unto us exceeding great and precious promises: that by these ye might be partakers of the divine nature, having escaped the corruption that is in the world through lust.

2 Peter 1:3-4

Once this earth suit dies, the spirit of man can no longer stay on the earth and would have to depart to the spirit world i.e. heaven or hell (as destined by his spiritual state at the time of the death of his human body).

We are confident, I say, and willing rather to be absent from the body, and to be present with the Lord.

2 Corinthians 5:8

But when we (the saints) shall see Jesus Christ return for His Bride/Church our physical bodies shall be supernaturally transformed into a spiritual body like the one our Lord and saviour Jesus Christ has. This is the full salvation of the body.

Behold, I show you a mystery; We shall not all sleep, but we shall all be changed,
In a moment, in the twinkling of an eye, at the last trump: for the trumpet shall
sound, and the dead shall be raised incorruptible, and we shall be changed.
For this corruptible must put on incorruption, and this mortal must put on
immortality.
So when this corruptible shall have put on incorruption, and this mortal shallhave
put on immortality, then shall be brought to pass the saying that is written,
Death is swallowed up in victory.

1 Corinthians 15:51-54

TEST YOURSELF
CHAPTER 6 – THE DYNAMICS OF MAN

The answer sheet is provided at the back of this manual.

1. The new recreated man whose spirit is restored back to God is one who:

    a) Looks different from others.
    b) Portrays good habits to his/her community.
    c) Goes to church and reads the word.
    d) Has God dwelling in Him as His temple.

2. The part of man that has God consciousness and is in touch with spiritual realities is:

    a) The spirit.
    b) The body.
    c) The feelings.
    d) The soul.

3. The self-conscious part of man is his:

    a) Spirit.
    b) Body.
    c) Temperament.
    d) Soul.

4. Man's soul does not get saved instantly at salvation and must therefore undergothree processes in order to effect the purpose of salvation of the soul. They are the _____, submitting of the will and taming of the emotions.

5. Man's _____ is the casing that gives him legal grounds to operate and function on the earth.

CHAPTER 7:

THE NEW CREATION

A New Creature

Therefore if any man be in Christ, he is a new creature: old things are passed away; behold all things are become new.

2 Corinthians 5:17

The phrase "if anyone is in Christ" implies that there are those both those in Christ and those outside Christ. However this word with its benefits and consequences only relates to those in Christ, these are those who have become members of the family of God and citizens of God's Kingdom by having accepted Jesus Christ as their Lord and Saviour. They have become new creatures i.e. a new species of being never seen before. They are born of the Spirit of God and recreated anew. The life of God having being imparted into their spirit by the Spirit of God, the Spirit of God recreates their human spirit into a new creature restored back into the image and likeness of God.

Jesus answered and said unto him, Verily, verily, I say unto thee, Except a man be born again, he cannot see the kingdom of God.
Jesus answered, Verily, verily, I say unto thee, Except a man be born of water and of the Spirit, he cannot enter into the kingdom of God.
That which is born of the flesh is flesh; and <u>that which is born of the Spirit</u> *(the Holy Spirit of God)* **is spirit** *(a new human spirit)*.

John 3:3 & :5-6

They experience a new dimension of life whereby all things pass away in split seconds as they become completely new creatures in the sight of God. This is the reason why Apostle Paul in his ministry says "I have wronged no man" (2 Corinthians 7:2). Was he denying that he had killed and persecuted the saints and Stephen? Was he saying that he was not the one behind all those threats to the church? No, but he was testifying to the newness inside him that had washed his old nature away. All things had become new. It was also the declaration of the beginning of a new life in Christ.

The changes that take place during the born again process may not necessarily be noticed on the outside due to the fact that the change is first within. It is our spirit being that instantly becomes new during the process. It receives of the life (Zoe) of God and is reconfigured into the image and likeness of God. It puts on the nature of God's being. It becomes a new creature, no more having the nature of sin inherited by Adam when he sinned against God, but now inheriting the nature of God, a righteous nature just as God is righteous in nature. This is part of what it means to be restored back into the image and likeness of God.

41

For he hath made him to be sin for us, who knew no sin; that <u>we might be made the righteousness of God in him</u>.

2 Corinthians 5:21

This causes us to take on certain new identities in life. These are:

A child of God

But as many as received him, to them gave he power *(authority/right)* **to become the sons of God, even to them that believe on his name**

John 1:12

For ye have not received the spirit of bondage again to fear; but ye have received the Spirit of adoption, whereby we cry, Abba, Father.
The Spirit itself beareth witness with our spirit, that we are the children of God:

Romans 8:15-16

When we confess Jesus Christ as our Lord and Saviour a spiritual reconfiguration takes place as we are transformed from the inside and hence the Spirit of God bears witness (evidence) with our own spirit that we are the children of God. We are immediately adopted and grafted into the family of God even as we put on God's divine nature. We are given the authority to become sons of God. We are God's children as we now have His Life (Zoe) and nature.

For God so loved the world, that he gave his only begotten Son, that whosoever believeth in him should not perish, but <u>have everlasting life</u> *(Zoe - the God Life)*.

John 3:16

According as <u>his divine power</u> hath given unto us all things that pertain unto life and godliness, through the knowledge of him that hath called us to glory and virtue:
Whereby are given unto us exceeding great and precious promises: that by these ye might be <u>partakers of the divine nature</u>, having escaped the corruption that is in the world through lust.

2 Peter 1:3-4

Any creature born of the Spirit of God will have the nature and the life of God. This is from the law of creation that says "like begets like" (Genesis 1:11-12). A mango tree brings forth mango fruit. A Donkey gives birth to a baby donkey. A lion does not give birth to a Giraffe, but rather to a lion cub. Likewise, a man gives birth to a man and a God (a mighty ruler) gives birth to little god (a mighty ruler) like creatures. Our spirits when we become born again are reborn of God's spirit, while our human flesh is born from our earthly Parents human flesh.

That which is born of the flesh is flesh; and <u>that which is born of the Spirit</u> *(the Holy Spirit of God)* **is spirit** *(a new human spirit)*.

John 3:6

This is why Jesus was referred to both as Son of God (of the God kind) and son of man (human). This meant He was both God's child, and a human being. The new creature in Christ is also both a son of God (the human spirit) and son of man (the soul and physical body).

As earlier mentioned the sooner we receive Christ into our hearts certain changes take place. We are literally transformed into becoming the children of God as we receive Him. Just as the child of a lion is a lion and that of an elephant is an elephant, so the child of God (a mighty ruler) is a god (a mighty ruler). Thus we qualify to become children of God in all rights. We now share the very nature of God, His life flows in us, His thoughts flow through us, His words become our words. Like a little child growing, we begin to orient ourselves into the ways of God through His nature that is like a seed in us.

The thief cometh not, but for to steal, and to kill, and to destroy: <u>I am come that they might have life, and that they might have it more abundantly</u>.

John 10:10

And that ye put on the new man *(new creature/human spirit)*, **which after God is created in righteousness and true holiness.**

Ephesians 4:24

For who hath known the mind of the Lord, that he may instruct him? But we have the mind of Christ.

1 Corinthians 2:16

For God hath not given us the spirit of fear; but of power, and of love, and of a sound mind.

2 Timothy 1:7

But speaking the truth in love, may grow up into him in all things, which is the head, even Christ:

Ephesians 4:15

As newborn babes, desire the sincere milk of the word, that ye may grow thereby:

1 Peter 2:2

The Jews got angry with Jesus because He called himself the Son of God which meant that He was a member of the God family. Yet Jesus further backed it by quoting from Psalm 82 concerning us who are children of God (a mighty ruler) being referred to as gods (mighty rulers) in the scripture (men were made by God to walk the earth like gods, representing the heavenly Father. But man fell from this position of glory and grace).

Therefore the Jews sought the more to kill him, because he not only had broken the sabbath, but <u>said also that God was his Father</u>, making himself equal with God.

John 5:18

The Jews answered him, saying, For a good work we stone thee not; but for blasphemy; and because that thou, being a man, makest thyself God.
Jesus answered them, Is it not written in your law, I said, Ye are gods?

John 10:33-34

I have said, Ye are gods; and all of you are children of the most High.

Psalm 82:6

This transition is more than a religious shift; we become princes in the Kingdom of God. We rule and reign with Him. We are nursed of Him and brought up by Him. As children of God we become His property and responsibility just like every parent is responsible for his or her child. As children of God we have rights in God's Kingdom because God is our Father, we also bear responsibility to advance the Fathers' business. We have the right to use His name, the right to be protected by Him, the right to be blessed etc. We become heirs of God and joint heirs with Christ. This means everything Christ has we also have equal access to.

The Spirit itself beareth witness with our spirit, that we are the children of God:
And if children, then heirs; heirs of God, and joint-heirs with Christ; if so be that we suffer with him, that we may be also glorified together.

Romans 8:16-17

Therefore let no man glory in men. For all things are yours;
Whether Paul, or Apollos, or Cephas, or the world, or life, or death, or things present, or things to come; all are yours;
And ye are Christ's; and Christ is God's.

1 Corinthians 3:21-23

Christ in us

For ye are all the children of God by faith in Christ Jesus.
For as many of you as have been baptized into Christ have put on Christ.
There is neither Jew nor Greek, there is neither bond nor free, there is neither male nor female: for ye are all one in Christ Jesus.

Galatians 3:26-28

In the early church a time came in Antioch as seen in Acts 11:26 when the disciples of Christ (those who studied and lived by the teachings of Jesus Christ) were first called "Christians". This word "Christian" meant "little Christ, Christ like, or followers of Christ". This name was given not only because the early saints spoke about Jesus the Christ and His teachings, but also because they manifested like Him.

True to this name, we who believe and confess His name should manifest like the Christ. The word Christ was not the surname of Jesus. It was simply a name designating His function. The word Christ means "the anointed one and His anointing". Jesus was anointed by God the Father through the Holy Spirit to accomplish the purposes of God on the earth (Isaiah 61:1-3 & Luke 4:18-21).

How God anointed Jesus of Nazareth with the Holy Ghost and with power: who went about doing good, and healing all that were oppressed of the devil; for God was with him.

Acts10:38

The anointing is not a feeling, a shaking, or a wind, but it is simply the empowerment of God upon any creature. It is God putting His ability upon another creature so that that creature can walk and work in the ability of God, and get results like God. This can give one the ability to love like God, to think and reason like God, to walk in and manifest the power of God, etc. Such a creature would end up getting results like God would on the earth. Therefore it is an endowment upon man or any other creature from the Most High God. We receive this ability to some dimension when we accept Jesus Christ as our Lord and saviour and become born again in Him, but we also are baptised into a greater dimension of God's life and endowment when we get baptised with the Holy Ghost/Spirit of God just like the disciples of Jesus Christ did in Acts 2. More on this shall be taught in later chapters of this book (The Holy Ghost, and Baptism in the Holy Ghost).

And when he had said this, he breathed on them, and saith unto them, Receive ye the Holy Ghost:

John 20:22

But ye shall receive power, after that the Holy Ghost is come upon you: and ye shall be witnesses unto me both in Jerusalem, and in all Judaea, and in Samaria, and unto the uttermost part of the earth.

Acts 1:8

According as his divine power hath given unto us all things that pertain unto life and godliness, through the knowledge of him that hath called us to glory and virtue:
Whereby are given unto us exceeding great and precious promises: that by these ye might be partakers of the divine nature, having escaped the corruption that is in the world through lust.

2 Peter 1:3-4

This is the change that happened to us the minute we receive of the life and the Spirit of God. This life of God imparted by the Holy Spirit changes us into a new creature (our spirit being), a creature that is now made of the very life of God. This life of God brings us into becoming members of God's family. We are now able to function like God on the earth, just like a baby lion would grow up to function like an adult lion. God has empowered us with His ability having restored us back into His image and likeness. This life of God and new nature allows us to be pure and holy like God, love like God, think and reason like God, and walk in the power of God. This new being we have become causes us to function like gods on the earth. Not forgetting that with the baptism of the Holy Ghost we are boosted to flow in an even greater dimension of this God likeness, as the Holy Ghost brings the Almightiness of God to work in our lives.

Then he answered and spake unto me, saying, This is the word of the LORD untoZerubbabel, saying, Not by might, nor by power, but by my spirit, saith the LORDof hosts.

Zechariah 4:6

This enables us to do the works of God on the earth as though God were the one doing it. Not by our power or might but by His ability working through us. This is also referred to as the grace of God. It is the endowment of God upon and within us, which causes us to function like God (His ambassadors) on this earth.

I am crucified with Christ: nevertheless I live; yet not I, <u>but Christ liveth in me</u>: and the life which I now live in the flesh I live by the faith of the Son of God, who loved me, and gave himself for me.

Galatians 2:20

Herein is our love made perfect, that we may have boldness in the day of judgment: <u>because as he is, so are we in this world</u>.

1 John 4:17

We become christs' because we are also anointed of God, having received of the Holy Spirit and the life of God within us. Hence, the scriptures say it is Christ that lives within us, and this is the hope of glory we have been waiting for. It is that new creature called Christ within you that God will use to demonstrate His glory and purposes unto the inhabitants of the earth.

Verily, verily, I say unto you, He that believeth on me, the works that I do shall he do also; and greater works than these shall he do; because I go unto my Father.

John 14:12

And saviours shall come up on mount Zion to judge the mount of Esau; and the kingdom shall be the LORD'S.

Obadiah 1:21

This is one of the reasons why Jesus Christ said that we would do the works he did and even greater works. The Bible also refers to us as saviours, because God would use us to deliver others from sin and death, and reconcile them to Him even as we do the works of Christ on the earth.

The reality of Christ in you becomes the glory of this new creature. This is His nature, mind/wisdom, power, grace, anointing, e,t,c. In Colossians 1:26 the Apostle Paul explains how the mystery (hidden wisdom of God) was hidden for ages but is now made manifest to the saints. The more we behold and are conscious of this wisdom of God the more we will bring forth this glory within us. Thus our lives become mirrors through which Christ is reflected to the world.

Even the mystery which hath been hid from ages and from generations, but now is made manifest to his saints:
To whom God would make known what is the riches of the glory of this mystery among the Gentiles; <u>which is Christ in you</u>, <u>the hope of glory</u>

Colossians 1:26-27

The more we grow in God then the more we are made perfect and grow in Christ, manifesting to greater degrees of His image and likeness. This is done as we also study (feed on) God's word, discovering the reality of who we have become in Christ Jesus.

Whom we preach, warning every man, and teaching every man in all wisdom; thatwe may present every man perfect in Christ Jesus:

Colossians 1:28

But speaking the truth in love, may grow up into him in all things, which is the head, even Christ:

Ephesians 4:15

As newborn babes, desire the sincere milk of the word, that ye may grow thereby:
1 Peter 2:2

But we all, with open face beholding as in a glass the glory of the Lord, are changed into the same image from glory to glory, even as by the Spirit of the Lord.

2 Corinthians 3:18

We should therefore now grow to walk in this earth as His reflection and representatives in the earth, radiating the glory of God in the earth. This is how the earth shall be filled with the glory of God, even as we continually reflect His glory in the earth.

Hath in these last days spoken unto us by his Son, whom he hath appointed heir of all things, by whom also he made the worlds;
Who <u>being the brightness of his glory, and the express image of his person</u>, and upholding all things by the word of his power, when he had by himself purged our sins, sat down on the right hand of the Majesty on high;

Hebrews 1:2-3

For the earth shall be filled with the knowledge of the glory of the Lord, as the waters cover the sea.

Habakkuk 2:14

TEST YOURSELF
CHAPTER 7 – THE NEW CREATION

The answer sheet is provided at the back of this manual.

1. We become new creatures:

   a) At biological birth.
   b) At resurrection.
   c) When we get born again.
   d) When we do many good works.

2. Which of the following is a reality of becoming a new creature?

   a) We are changed from the outside in.
   b) We are changed from the inside out.
   c) We receive a new life after some years in the Lord.
   d) We lose touch of this world and become funny people.

3. Which of the following is true concerning the name "Christ"?

   a) It was the surname of Jesus.
   b) It refers to the anointed one and His anointing.
   c) It is the name given by the angel to Elizabeth, Mary's cousin.
   d) None of the above.

4. The reality of Christ in you becomes the _____ of this new creature.

5. It is the new creature called _____ within you that God will use to demonstrate His glory and purposes unto the inhabitants of the earth.

CHAPTER 8:

PURPOSE

Everything has a purpose

Every creation of God was created for a purpose. God had a reason for which it was made. It was made to fulfil God's will and for God's pleasure.

Thou art worthy, O Lord, to receive glory and honour and power: for thou hast created all things, and <u>for thy pleasure they are and were created</u>.

Revelation 4:11

Who is the image of the invisible God, the firstborn of every creature:
For by him were all things created, that are in heaven, and that are in earth, visible and invisible, whether they be thrones, or dominions, or principalities, or powers: <u>all things were created by him, and for him</u>:

Colossians 1:15-16

Where the purpose for anything is not known then abnormal use or misuse cannot be avoided. It can also lead to perversion. Until the purpose for anything created is discovered, the full potential of that thing will never be attained. The best person from whom to find the true purpose of a thing is not the thing itself but the creator of the thing. The creator or manufacturer of a thing is the best person who can tell the original intent or purpose for the thing. For instance, many do not utilize their electric gadgets (like video cassette players) to the fullest. They take the player out of the box not bothering to read the manufacturer's manual and miss out on latest technological additions that give additional benefits and also make operating the machine easier. Therefore, they do not enjoy its full potential.

God has a unique purpose for you

Likewise, not only does God have a general purpose for man (which is to worship, reflect, and serve God), but God also has a unique purpose for every man born into the earth. While we know that we are all made to worship, reflect, and serve God as already taught in an earlier chapter, yet we all have a unique area of service that God has ordained to use us in.

God's unique purpose for you is God's agenda or programme for you during your time on the earth. It is God's plan (will or blueprint) for you and not your plan for yourself. It cannot be compared to any grandeur plan that you or anyone can have for you. God will not use every one as an Apostle, Prophet, Pastor, Evangelist, or Teacher. God may use some of us in business, some in education, some in government, some in entertainment, etc. And even in these diverse areas we will still all have unique ways in which God will use us to serve Him.

For we are his workmanship, created in Christ Jesus unto good works, which God Hath before ordained that we should walk in them.

Ephesians 2:10

There is a unique reason for which each of us exists on the earth today, and for which God has designed and desired to use us in fulfilling His good will and purposes on the earth. God's purpose for us is always good and the best purpose for us because it was designed according to His infinite and manifold wisdom.

In whom also we have obtained an inheritance, being predestinated according to the purpose of him who worketh all things after the counsel of his own will:

Ephesians 1:11

Before I formed thee in the belly I knew thee, and before thou camest forth out of womb I sanctified thee, and I ordained thee...

Jeremiah 1:5

God set every man's destiny according to His designed purpose and will for that particular man, yet it is up to men to choose to fulfil God's purpose for their lives. We can choose God's designed purpose for us, or choose our own designed destiny (also known as ambition), or the devil's designed destiny for our lives. It is ultimately up to every man to decide which designed destiny would be fulfilled in his/her life. Jesus chose to fulfil God's designed destiny and will for Him during His earthly ministry, while Adam and Eve chose their own destiny and aborted God's ordained purpose and destiny for them.

It is a pity that many people never get to discover and fulfil their God ordained purposes before they die. Till date, it is a very small percentage of believers that both discover and fulfil their God-ordained purpose in their lifetime. We must develop our priestly ministry and an intimate walk with God so that we can learn to hear from the one (God) who has designed our true purpose, as it is He who will reveal our true purpose to our hearts and our minds.

But as it is written, Eye hath not seen, nor ear heard, neither have entered into the heart of man, the things which God hath prepared for them that love him.
But God hath revealed them unto us by his Spirit: for the Spirit searcheth all things, yea, the deep things of God.

1 Corinthians 2:9-10

Vision

The use of the word "Vision" here means "having God given insight into God's purposes for your life".

And the LORD answered me, and said, Write the vision, and make it plain upon tables, that he may run that readeth it.

Habakkuk 2:2

This type of vision should not be confused with the spiritual visions where God allows men to see into the spiritual world. Neither should it be mistaken to be representing human ambition or pursuits. Ambition refers to a person's personal designed goals, dreams and pursuits in life. They are personal goals and dreams that have been influenced by several factors such as ones environment, family background, peer pressure, the world e.t.c, and was not necessarily designed by God. Though the world calls this vision, yet in the kingdom of God we call it ambition.

Vision is continuously unfolding with time. It is the continuous discovery of God's purposes for our life on the earth. The more we discover our purpose the more we have vision. Vision is hence never entered into from the top, but rather we grow into it and in it. We make advancement and progress in fulfilling God's vision for us a step at a time. God orders our steps into the fulfilment of His purposes for us. It is purpose per time, or growing into the fulfilment of His ultimate purpose for us as we follow the blueprint God has for our lives.

Then said I, Lo, I come (in the volume of the book it is written of me,) to do thy will, O God.

Hebrews 10:7

True success in life is measured by our fulfilment of God's purposes and vision for us on the earth, and not just by how much wealth, fame, and influence we gain on the earth.

Jesus saith unto them, My meat is to do the will of him that sent me, and to finish his work.

John 4:34

Calling

This refers to God's divine request towards us to fulfil our God designed and ordained purposes. Every believer is called to fulfil God's purpose for his or her life.

And we know that all things work together for good to them that love God, to them who are the called according to his purpose.

Romans 8:28

We are limited to fulfilling our calling by how much of it we see per time (vision) and our level of obedience to walk with God faithfully to the end, no matter the pressures of life (contradictory situations, devilish attacks, and persecutions) and pleasures of life (the good things of this earth and life) that come our way.

Gifting/Talent

God never sends a person on a divine assignment without first equipping the person with the ability to carry out the divine task at hand. It is primarily for this reason that God has carefully designed and fabricated every single individual and equipped us with divers abilities specially suited for our unique individual purposes or assignments on the earth. They are the endowment of God's ability upon men so that men can function like God on the earth. God is multi-gifted and talented and expresses His diverse gifts and talents through us all. After all we are made in God's image to function like God. It is because God sings that we sing, etc.God carefully and wonderfully made our unique personalities (this does not include our character flaws) and our unique gifting and talents, for our unique purpose.

For thou hast possessed my reins: thou hast covered me in my mother's womb. I will praise thee, for I am fearfully and wonderfully made: marvellous are thy works, and that my soul knoweth right well.

Psalms 139:13-14

God gives to us of His multitalented abilities so that we can function like Him on the earth and get His work done. These talents and abilities can be observed in us from a young age and can be developed with time and practice. They are divine endowments that are resident in the person just waiting to be discovered. When properly understood and used, they work as strengths that we use to be productive on the earth and influence God's dominion on the earth.

And God blessed (empowered) **them, and God said unto them, Be fruitful, and multiply, and replenish the earth, and subdue it: and have dominion over the fish of the sea, and over the fowl of the air, and over every living thing that moveth upon the earth.**

Genesis 1:28

Nations of calling

Every one of us is called to serve God in and some specific area(s) of calling on the earth.

And Jesus came and spake unto them, saying, All power is given unto me in heaven and in earth.
Go ye therefore, and teach all nations, baptizing them in the name of the Father,and of the Son, and of the Holy Ghost:

Teaching them to observe all things whatsoever I have commanded you: and, lo, Iam with you alway, even unto the end of the world. Amen.

Matthew 28:18-20

Jesus Christ charged His Church on the earth with this divine commission. We are to reach out into all the nations of the earth and bring them all back into the state in which God originally created and intended them to exist in before the fall of man. This is to bring them back into God's original purpose (to worship, reflect, and serve God), will (blueprint, agenda, and plan), righteousness (order, etc), and standard of excellence in which He intended for them to operate in before the fall of man. We are to seek this till they are all brought back under the influence of God's Kingdom.

The word "nations" in Matthew 28:19 is from the Greek word "Ethnos" which means "habit" or "race". It refers to a community of people who have or share certain things in common. Some of the different similarities that the people who make up a community may share in common can range from:

1. People having a common language (criteria used for defining a nation in the first early world. E.g. Luo, Kikuyu, Greek, Roman, Anglo-Saxon, etc.). These are called the **language-based or ethnic-based nations**.

2. People who reside within or share a common geographical boundary (E.g. Kenya, USA, Great Britain, China, Australia, Equador,e.t.c). These are called the **geography-based nations**.

3. People who work in a common profession or industry, meaning that they share a common profession or craft (E.g. The nation of religion such as the Vatican, the nation or world of sports, etc). These are called the **professional-based nations, mountains of culture, professional worlds, market-place, sectors of industry, or spheres of society**.

Hence when Jesus said to His Church in Mathew 28:18-20 to go and reconcile the nations/world to God as in 2 Corinthians 5:18-19, He was not only telling us to go into our geographical and language based nations/worlds, but to also reach out to reconcile our professional nations/worlds to God.

The seven major professional nations/worlds which can be further broken down into smaller categories include:

I) The World/Nation of Religion (Life-givers). This includes all those called into the five-fold ministry offices (e.g. the Apostles, Prophets, Evangelists, Pastors, and Teachers), those who support the five-fold offices through the ministry of helps (e.g. ushers, praise leaders, etc), and those in health-care (e.g. medical doctors, pharmacists, medical scientists, medical support personnel, herbal healers,etc).

II) The World/Nation of Industry, Commerce, and Finance.

III) The Family Institution.

IV) The World/Nation of Arts, Media, and Entertainment.

V) The World/Nation of Science, Technology, and Education.

VI) The World/Nation of Government and Military. This covers the professional worlds/spheres of the executive arm of government (including the civil service), the judicial arm of government (including the legal fraternity), the legislative arm of government, non-governmental organizations, social services, all the disciplined forces, and the security institutions or professions (both government and private owned).

VII) The World/Nation of Sports.
No one person can reach into all these professional-based nations alone. We are all diversely and uniquely gifted to reach out to and through one or more of these worlds, letting the light (grace and ability) of Christ shine through us as we do His good and great works (Matthew 5:13-16). This way people would be attracted to God's light in us and we will reconcile them back to God. This is bringing them back into God's original purpose, will, righteousness (order, etc), and standards of excellence for each of them.

TEST YOURSELF
CHAPTER 8 – PURPOSE

The answer sheet is provided at the back of this manual.

1. Every creation of God was created for a purpose which is:

   a) To enjoy life.
   b) To become famous.
   c) To fulfil God's will and pleasure.
   d) To have riches.

2. We find out the true purpose of our lives by:

   a) Asking other people.
   b) Spending time with God.
   c) Attending seminars.
   d) Reading books.

3. Which one of the following does not make reference to the term nations?

   a) People called to a particular community.
   b) People who share a common industry or profession.
   c) People who share a common geographical boundary.
   d) People who share similar views in life.

4. The term vision means -

   _____.

5. God never sends a person on a divine assignment without first _____ the person with the ability to carry out the divine task at hand.

CHAPTER 9:

THE WORD OF GOD

God the word

Jesus Christ is God the Word. He is the Word of God that became flesh.

In the beginning was the Word, and the Word was with God, and the Word was God.
The same was in the beginning with God.
All things were made by him; and without him was not any thing made that wasmade.

John 1:1-3

He is also part of the trinity known as the God-head (The Father, the Word, and the Holy Spirit).

For there are three that bear record in heaven, the Father, <u>the Word</u>, and the HolyGhost: and these three are one.

1 John 5:7

The Word was even before the beginning of time, was with God, and was God. All things were made by the Word and for God. Yet when the Father sent Him into the earth for the redemption of man he took not an angelic body but rather a human body and was named Jesus the Christ. He became the Word of God personified. The Word incarnate or the Word became flesh.

The spoken word

The spoken word of God is the word that proceeds (comes out) from the mouth of God.

But he answered and said, It is written, Man shall not live by bread alone, but by every word that proceedeth out of the mouth of God.

Matthew 4:4

God speaks to us through diverse ways, ranging from His still small voice on our inside, visions and dreams, to words of prophecy through other God inspired people, etc.

God, who at sundry times and in divers manners spake in time past unto the fathers by the Prophets,

Hebrews 1:1

God expects us to live by His word. When we live by God's word we shall make our way prosperous and have good success. It is by cooperating with God and His ways that He will show us how to prosper and go ahead in every area of life.

Thus saith the LORD, thy Redeemer, the Holy One of Israel; I am the LORD thy God which teacheth thee to profit, which leadeth thee by the way that thou shouldest go.

Isaiah 48:17

The written word

The written word of God, which has been compiled into a book known as the Bible, is our manual for living. It is the inspired written word of God. It was the Holy Ghost who inspired holy men of God to write the scriptures, which were compiled into today's New and Old Testament Bible.

Knowing this first, that no prophecy of the scripture is of any private interpretation.
For the prophecy came not in old time by the will of man: but holy men of God spake as they were moved by the Holy Ghost.

2 Peter 1:20-21

The manufacturers of many electronic products sell their products with a product manual, which is a handbook that shows the buyer relevant information to properly use, maintain, and sometimes repair the product if it gets damaged. Likewise, God being the creator (like a manufacturer) of man has also written the Bible as the product manual for man. It shows you why man was made, how man is to operate on the earth, what to do to avoid malfunctioning, the best environment within which to operate, etc. The Bible also has troubleshooting sections, to help deal with any signs of malfunctioning.

God has set it such that we learn more of His ways and His thoughts through the knowledge of His written word. Indeed it has been given to us for our profiting, because it reveals the nature, person, and ways of God to us. In it we learn principles that help equip us to fulfil our God ordained purpose in life, develop us into our full potential in Christ, and to access and enjoy our full inheritance in Christ both on this earth and in the life to come. It carries God's wisdom for every area of our life. There is nothing that the word of God does not provide wisdom for handling or dealing with.

The life transforming power of the Word

For the word of God is quick, and powerful, and sharper than any two-edged sword, piercing even to the dividing asunder of soul and spirit, and of the joints and marrow, and is a discerner of the thoughts and intents of the heart.

Hebrews 4:12

It is clear from the above scripture that the word of God is powerful enough to divide the body, soul, and spirit of man. It does not suffer any limitations as its power transcends all barriers. The word of God transcends into every area of man with its life transforming power. It is used to shape and perfect the believer in Christ Jesus.

To whom God would make known what is the riches of the glory of this mystery among the Gentiles; which is Christ in you, the hope of glory:
Whom we preach, warning every man, and teaching every man in all wisdom; that we may present every man perfect in Christ Jesus:

Colossians 1:27-28

It profits us in diverse ways and areas whenever we have a good grasp of it and apply it in our lives.

All scripture is given by inspiration of God, and is profitable for <u>doctrine</u>, for <u>reproof</u>, for <u>correction</u>, for <u>instruction in righteousness</u>: That the man of God may be perfect, thoroughly furnished unto all good works.

2 Timothy 3:16-17

From the scripture in 2 Timothy 3:16-17 we can derive that the scriptures are profitable to us in the following ways:

1. It establishes us in sound doctrine and the truth of God's word. It is our yard stick for us to judge what sound doctrine is, lest we go off into error. It is the more sure word of prophecy with which we judge every other manifestation of God's word.

We have also a more sure word of prophecy; whereunto ye do well that ye take heed, as unto a light that shineth in a dark place, until the day dawn, and the day star arise in your hearts:
Knowing this first that no prophecy of the scripture is of any private interpretation.
For the prophecy came not in old time by the will of man: but holy men of God spake as they were moved by the Holy Ghost.

2 Peter 1:19-21

This means even if we receive a manifestation of the person of the word (Jesus Christ) or the spoken word (the voice of God) it should be judged by the rightly divided word of God. If it does not measure up to the word of God then we should put aside whatever revelation or instruction we have received no matter the glory of the presentation with which it came to us.

But though we, or an angel from heaven, preach any other gospel unto you than that which we have preached unto you, let him be accursed.
As we said before, so say I now again, If any man preach any other gospel unto you than that ye have received, let him be accursed.

Galatians 1:8-9

2. It is the evidence of God's Kingdom used as a tool in the hand of the believer. It is evidence of God and His Kingdom which is used to rebuke and resist the devil, so as to destroy or undo the works of the Kingdom of darkness. It is this word of God when skilfully and rightly applied that is used to establish God's Kingdom on the earth and to destroy the works of darkness. It is used to convict the world and believers of the reality of God and His Kingdom (Titus 1:9 & Jude 1:14-15). It also teaches us how to enjoy and experience our salvation in Christ Jesus. We see Jesus using the word of God to resist Satan when he was tempted of Satan in the wilderness.

Then saith Jesus unto him, Get thee hence, Satan: for it is written, Thou shalt worship the Lord thy God, and him only shalt thou serve.
Then the devil leaveth him, and, behold, angels came and ministered unto him.
Matthew 4:10-11

The word of God carries the irresistible power of God. There is nothing that can withstand the power of God's word because all things (spiritual, soulical, and physical) were made by that word. The power of God goes forth to confirm His word in any situation when applied as we see in Mark 16:20. It is this same work of God or the principles/truth hidden in it that set us free when applied rightly in our lives.

Then said Jesus to those Jews which believed on him, If ye continue in my word, then are ye my disciples indeed;
And ye shall know the truth, and the truth shall make you free.
John 8:31-32

3. It is used to correct the believer in his ways. It shines as a bright light in our hearts, bringing us into an understanding of God's ways and will. It shines as a lamp to our feet and a light to our path, thereby hindering us from sliding and making mistakes.

Thy word is a lamp unto my feet, and a light unto my path.
Psalm 119:105

It is therefore the rod of correction of our heavenly Father. Even when we want to correct one another we are to use the word of God.

Let the word of Christ dwell in you richly in all wisdom; teaching and admonishing one another in psalms and hymns and spiritual songs, singing with grace in your hearts to the Lord.
Colossians 3:16

4. It acts as the standard to train the believer in the right ways of God. It teaches us about the righteousness of God which is of a different and higher standard from the righteousness of the world around us.

I (wisdom) lead in the way of righteousness, in the midst of the paths of judgment:
Proverbs 8:20

Studying The Word

The only way the Word of God will benefit and bring profit into the life of a person is when we discover it and then rightly apply it to our lives.

1. Discover it.

Study to show thyself approved unto God, a workman that needeth not to be ashamed, rightly dividing the word of truth.

2 Timothy 2:15

Every believer in Christ who does not want to be ashamed in the day or hour of need, ought to study the word of God and learn to rightly divide it. It is when we study and read through the word of God that we become familiar and knowledgeable about its contents. This way we get the accurate knowledge (information) of God's word.

We then begin to ponder over and reason on what we have read in the scriptures so as to get understanding or insight into their meaning. This is called meditation. Understanding can also be obtained through the explanation and teaching of the word of God by others. This can be done by listening to video or audio messages on the word of God, reading books on the word of God, and attending services, seminars and conferences where the word of God is being taught.

Proper understanding (insight) into the working of God's word will then make us skilful on how to properly apply the principles hidden in the scriptures in our everyday lives. We must gather knowledge (information), understanding (insight), and wisdom (right application) of the various principles (also known as truths) which are hidden in the scriptures. This is what it means to be able to rightly divide the word of God. It is not just cramming them into our minds, but knowing how to practically and rightly apply them in our lives.

Let the word of Christ <u>dwell in you richly in all wisdom</u>; teaching and admonishing one another in psalms and hymns and spiritual songs, singing with grace in your hearts to the Lord.

Colossians 3:16

2. Apply it

The word of God needs to be applied in order for it to profit us. The principles discovered in God's word must be diligently and rightly applied in order for its profit to appear.

Meditate upon these things; <u>give thyself wholly to them</u>; that thy profiting may appear to all.

1 Timothy 4:15

Applying the word of God is comparable to the planting of a seed. A seed is useless in your hand if it is not planted, it needs to be planted in order for it to bring forth its fruit, and therefore the word of God only works for us when we rightly apply it. Remember also that it is the principles (also known as truths) in God's word which when we rightly apply brings forth results or fruits.

Then said Jesus to those Jews which believed on him, If ye continue in my word, then are ye my disciples indeed;
And ye shall know the truth, and the truth shall make you free.

John 8:31-32

Therefore when we study God's word, if we want to see and enjoy its full profit we must endeavour to take time to diligently apply itby our relevant speech and/or actions. We must not be like those who after hearing God's word forget what they have heard and the word does not profit them. It is not those who hear the word that are blessed but rather those who both have heard and apply the same rightly into their lives.

For if any be a hearer of the word, and not a doer, he is like unto a man beholding his natural face in a glass:
For hebeholdeth himself, and goeth his way, and straightway forgetteth what manner of man he was.
But whoso looketh into the perfect law of liberty, and continueth therein, he beingnot a forgetful hearer, but a doer of the work, this man shall be blessed in hisdeed.

James 1:23-25

TEST YOURSELF
CHAPTER 9 – THE WORD OF GOD

The answer sheet is provided at the back of this manual.

1. The word of God is profitable to us in the following ways. Which one is not true?

   a) It establishes us in sound doctrine.
   b) For correction.
   c) For instruction in righteousness.
   d) It tells us that we shall live in heaven forever after life on earth.

2. The following statements are not true about how holy men came up with scriptures. Which one is true?

   a) The holy men discovered where the scriptures had been hidden by God.
   b) The Holy Ghost was inspired by holy men to write scriptures.
   c) Holy men through research found out about God and they put it in writing.
   d) The holy men were inspired by the Holy Ghost to write the scriptures.

3. Which of the following is not true concerning the word?

   a) It is Jesus Christ personified.
   b) It was the instrument that was used in the creation process.
   c) It is what man is to be continually sustained by and not by bread alone.
   d) It is what was written by men who had a religious experience.

4. Without discovering and _____ the word of God into our lives, our lives will not reflect any added value.

5. The word of God carries_____ for every area of our lives thus making it relevant in every stage and point in life.

CHAPTER 10:

THE HOLY SPIRIT

Who is the Holy Spirit?

The Holy Spirit is not a wind, fire or a feeling. Contrary to many differing beliefs on who the Holy Spirit is, simply put, He is the third person in the Godhead/Trinity.

For there are three that bear record in heaven, the Father, the Word, and <u>the Holy Ghost</u>: and these three are one.

1 John 5:7

It is important to note that just as God the Father and the Son are distinct persons so is God the Holy Spirit, yet the three are one. We see the Holy Spirit present even in the early days of Creation (Genesis 1:2). He was also involved in the decision making process of Creation (Genesis 1:26). Though all persons of the trinity are at work, the Holy Spirit is currently the more dominant feature amongst the Godhead at work in the affairs of men in the earth. The Holy Spirit is God as present and active in the spiritual experience of men. Thus the Holy Spirit is a person as well as God. We are presently in the age of the Holy Spirit because He is the person of the Godhead presently at work in the earth, and hence we should not be ignorant about His Deity and personality if we want to fully experience and enjoy God in the earth.

His role as the Comforter

After the death and resurrection of Christ, God the Holy Spirit took centre stage administrating the purposes of God on the earth through men. Jesus introduced the Holy Spirit to His disciples as he was preparing to leave the earth.

And I will pray the Father, and he shall give you another Comforter, that he may abide with you forever;
Even the Spirit of truth; whom the world cannot receive, because it seeth him not, neither knoweth him: but ye know him; for hedwelleth with you, and shall be in you.
I will not leave you comfortless: I will come to you.

John 14:16-18

But the Comforter, which is the Holy Ghost, whom the Father will send in my name, he shall teach you all things, and bring all things to your remembrance, whatsoever I have said unto you.

John 14:26

When Jesus Christ spoke out these words, He implied that the Father would send another Comforter to replace Him on the earth. The word another implies one who is equal to the one He has come to replace, yet different in person. This is because the Holy Ghost was coming to be to the disciples what Jesus was to them when He was present with them on the earth. This was to be an equal comforter. Equal in every aspect of being, yet a different person of the Trinity i.e. Equal in power (ability) and authority (Jurisdiction).

The Parakletos

The word Parakletos is the word comforter in the Greek language. The Holy Ghost is our Parakletos (John 14:16). The word Parakletos when carefully examined gives us a better understanding about the personality, strengths and ministry of the Holy Spirit. The Holy Spirit came to replace Jesus Christ as the person of the Godhead with an earthly ministry. He became everything that Jesus was to the disciples. He was to be their new Parakletos, just as Jesus had been a Parakletos to them. This meant that anytime they needed a Parakletos they were not to turn to Jesus but to the Holy Spirit. He was to be as real to them and at work in them as when Jesus was with them as their Parakletos.

A Parakletos is:

A Helper. He is a helper who helps us in our weakness just as Jesus was a helper who helped the disciples in their weaknesses. Romans 8:26.

A Standby. He is to stand by us and never leave us nor forsake us even as Jesus had done faithfully. 1 John 2:27 &1 Corinthians 3:16-17.

An Advocate. He is our advocate always ready and willing to stand in the gap and intercede on our behalf. Romans 8:26-27 &1 Corinthians 14:2.

A Strengthener. He is to continue to strengthen us even as Jesus had strengthened them. Ephesians 3:16 & Colossians 1:11.

A Guide. He is to guide us in all truth. He was to guide them just as Jesus had done. John 16:13, Isaiah 48:17, & Psalm 23.

A Teacher. He is to continue to teach us just as Jesus had. John 14:26, Isaiah 48:17 &1 John 2:27.

A Counselor. He is to give us counsel just as Jesus had given them. Isaiah 11:2.

A Consoler or Comforter. Just as God has always been a Comforter to man (Isaiah 51:12), likewise the Holy Spirit became the new Comforter, always available to comfort us. 2 Corinthians 1:3-4, John 14:26, &Isaiah 11:2

The fruit of the Spirit

But the fruit of the Spirit is love, joy, peace, longsuffering, gentleness, goodness, faith,
Meekness, temperance: against such there is no law.
And they that are Christ's have crucified the flesh with the affections and lusts.

Galatians 5:22-24

The fruit of the Spirit is the character or nature of God given by and through the Holy Spirit to men. It is a by-product of the Holy Spirit. They are godly habits produced in the life of the born-again believer. They are love, joy, peace, long-suffering, gentleness, goodness, faith, meekness and temperance.

It is only natural for the branches to produce fruit after the kind of the plant. As we stay connected to God through His Spirit, we find ourselves producing after His kind. There is a development process by which the fruit gets established in our life to the point it becomes a physical manifestation.

According as his divine power hath given unto us all things that pertain unto life and godliness, through the knowledge of him that hath called us to glory and virtue:
Whereby are given unto us exceeding great and precious promises: that by these ye might be partakers of the divine nature, having escaped the corruption that is in the world through lust.

2 Peter 1:3-4

Gifts of the Spirit

For to one is given by the Spirit the word of wisdom; to another the word of knowledge by the same Spirit;
To another faith by the same Spirit; to another the gifts of healing by the same Spirit;
To another the working of miracles; to another prophecy; to another discerning of spirits; to another divers kinds of tongues; to another the interpretation of tongues:

1 Corinthians 12:8-10

There are nine manifestations (sometime called the gifts) of the Holy Spirit recorded in scripture. These manifestations of the Spirit are special manifestations of the Holy Spirit who dwells (permanently) in any Christian who has been baptized in the Holy Spirit.

They are divine abilities or endowments manifested through the believer by the Spirit of God.

These nine manifestations of the Spirit of God may not be the only manifestations of the Spirit of God that there are, but these are simply those recorded in scripture by the Apostle Paul. They are: **the word of wisdom; the word of knowledge; faith; the gifts of healing; the working of miracles; prophecy; discerning of spirits; diverse kinds of tongues and the interpretation of tongues.**

Every manifestation of God will always bring glory to Him (God), and work towards and not against His eternal purposes. These gifts are used to conduct divine purposes and plans and hence establish God's Kingdom. It is also important to note that they are a means to an end and not an end in themselves. Since they come from the Holy Spirit, they are the ability of God given to us to get God kind of results in our everyday life.

The Giver of Ministry Graces

The Holy Spirit is also the one who empowers people to function in certain Kingdom offices on the earth. He imparts men and women with both the Five-fold ministry gifts/graces, and other graces needed to function and serve in other offices (within the different professional nations) in God's Kingdom on earth (1 Corinthians 12:27-29).

The Five fold ministry gifts are the Apostle, Prophet, Evangelist, Pastor and Teacher.

But unto every one of us is given grace according to the measure of the gift of Christ.
Wherefore he saith, When he ascended up on high, he led captivity captive, and gave gifts unto men.
(Now that he ascended, what is it but that he also descended first into the lower parts of the earth?
He that descended is the same also that ascended up far above all heavens, that he might fill all things.)
And he gave some, apostles; and some, prophets; and some, evangelists; and some, pastors and teachers;
For the perfecting of the saints, for the work of the ministry, for the edifying of the body of Christ:

Ephesians 4:7-12

Some of the other graces given in other areas of ministry are: Ruling, showing mercy, giving, etc. More of these graces are still being discovered and they are the different gifting or talents that relate to the different professional nations e.g. Administration, Singing etc.

Having then gifts differing according to the grace that is given to us, whether prophecy, let us prophesy according to the proportion of faith;
Or ministry, let us wait on our ministering: or he that teacheth, on teaching;

Or he that exhorteth, on exhortation: he that giveth, let him do it with simplicity; he that ruleth, with diligence; he that sheweth mercy, with cheerfulness.

Romans 12:6-8

TEST YOURSELF
CHAPTER 10 – THE HOLY SPIRIT

The answer sheet is provided at the back of this manual.

1. Which of the following is true about who the Holy Spirit is?

    a) A wind.
    b) A fire.
    c) A feeling.
    d) The third person of the trinity.

2. The Holy Spirit is our Parakletos. Which of the following is not His role as Parakletos?

    a) A guide.
    b) A teacher.
    c) A prophet.
    d) A counsellor.

3. Which of the following is a proper definition of the fruit of the Spirit?

    a) It is the character or nature of God given by and through the Holy Spirit to men.
    b) It is recommendable behaviours in a people.
    c) It is the equivalent of behavioural temperaments in people.
    d) It is the mastering of good traits from proper upbringing.

4. The five-fold ministry gifts are _____,prophet, evangelist, pastor, and teacher.

5. There are _____ manifestations (gifts) of the Holy Spirit as recorded in the Bible.

CHAPTER 11:

THE BAPTISM OF THE HOLY SPIRIT

The Baptism of the Holy Spirit

There is a difference between the Holy Spirit coming to dwell in a person immediately he/she becomes born-again, and the baptism of the Holy Ghost or infilling of the Holy Ghost. These are two different experiences that a born-again believer can have with the Holy Ghost.

The Salvation experience. Every born again believer in Christ has the Holy Ghost dwelling in him/her. We become the temples of God because the Holy Ghost dwells in us. It is this same Holy Spirit that initially imparts the life of God into the spirit man of the convert, causing him/her to become a new creature in Christ Jesus.

Know ye not that ye are the temple of God, and that the Spirit of God dwelleth in you?

1 Corinthians 3:16

The disciples/apostles experience of receiving the Holy Ghost in John 20:22 was a salvation experience, while the experience of receiving the Holy Ghost in Acts 2:1-4 was a baptism experience.

And when he had said this, he breathed on them, and saith unto them, Receive ye the Holy Ghost:

John 20:22

And when the day of Pentecost was fully come, they were all with one accord in one place.
And suddenly there came a sound from heaven as of a rushing mighty wind, and it filled all the house where they were sitting.
And there appeared unto them cloven tongues like as of fire, and it sat upon each of them.
And they were all filled with the Holy Ghost, and began to speak with other tongues, as the Spirit gave them utterance.

Acts 2:1-4

The Baptism experience. There is another experience of the infilling of the Holy Ghost called the baptism in the Holy Ghost. The word baptised means to be fully immersed or covered into. Therefore the baptism in the Holy Ghost means the full immersion of the believer into the Holy Ghost. This is where the Spirit of God brings or endows the believer with the fullness of God's ability/strengths in potential form. This fullness of God becomes resident in the believer, and brings the ability for the believer to manifest fully like God in the earth.

There are numerous instances in the scriptures where people got saved but were not yet baptised with the Holy Ghost, but got baptised much later. For example, the people of Samaria got born-again in Acts 8:12 and Acts 8:16, but got baptised in the Holy Ghost after the Apostles Peter and John were sent from Jerusalem to lay hands upon them in prayer in Acts 8:14-17. Jesus spoke of this experience of the baptism of the Holy Spirit as an experience of infilling of the Holy Ghost that would lead to an out flow of the life of God from the believer.

He that believeth on me, as the scripture hath said, out of his belly shall flow rivers of living water.
(But this spake he of the Spirit, which they that believe on him should receive: for the Holy Ghost was not yet given; because that Jesus was not yet glorified.)
John 7:38-39

A simple illustration which can be demonstrated or imagined by the reader of this book and used to show the difference between the salvation and the baptism experience of receiving the Holy Ghost in a believer is as follows: The salvation experience of receiving the Holy Ghost by a believer in Christ can be likened to if you pour some water (the water is typological of the Holy Ghost or the Life of God - Zoe) into a cup (representing the believer in Christ). The cup remains wet with some amount of water, though not filled to over flowing. Neither is the cup immersed or baptized with water. This shows how every born again believer in Christ has the Holy Ghost and the Life (Zoe) of God in them, though the believer at this stage is not necessarily baptized in the Holy Ghost. To demonstrate the baptism of the Holy Ghost experience in the life of a believer, you now need to fill a big jug (having a larger capacity than that of your cup) with water (again typological of the Holy Ghost and the Life of God - Zoe). Keep pouring the water from the jug into the cup and don't stop. Allow the water to not only fill the cup, but to also begin to spill out after it has been filled to the brim of the cup. The cup at this stage is filled over with water, which not only covers the cup, but also flows out of it, spilling to the ground (you can place a large bucket under the cup so as not to spill water on the floor). This is like the baptism experience that the scriptures describe in John 7:38-39, in which the believer, just like the cup is not only immersed (baptized) in the waters of Life (Zoe), but the water supplied from the jug into the cup also begins to flow out from the cup into the environment around the cup. This out flow of water both depicts the over flow of the Life of God (rivers of living waters) through the believer and the effect of the over flow that causes the believer to break forth into the speaking with other tongues. Now imagine if instead of a jug you had a wide pipe connecting a never-ending ocean to your cup. The water (typifying the Zoe or water of Life of God) will not only fill the room where you are carrying out this demonstration, but it would also fill and cover the whole planet earth. It will fill and cover the earth with the glory of God.

He that believeth on me, as the scripture hath said, out of his belly shall flow rivers of living water.

(But this spake he of the Spirit, which they that believe on him should receive: for the Holy Ghost was not yet given; because that Jesus was not yet glorified.)

John 7:38-39

For the earth shall be filled with the knowledge of the glory of the Lord, as the waters cover the sea.

Habakkuk 2:14

One of the signs or evidence of the baptism of the Holy Ghost in the life of a born-again believer is the speaking with new tongues. "Tongues" means languages. Here the believer can be inspired by the Holy Spirit to speak in divers (different) languages other than the language he or she knows naturally (1 Corinthians 12:8-11).

And these signs shall follow them that believe; In my name shall they cast out devils; they shall speak with new tongues;

Mark 16:17

According to the scriptures, there is yet another evidence of the baptism in the Holy Ghost in the life of the believer, and this is the speaking in what is called an "unknown tongue" (unknown language) which is speaking in a heavenly language. 1 Corinthians 13:1 tells us it is possible to speak or pray (talking of prayer in the context of scripture) in the tongues of men or of angels (heavenly language). The experience of praying in an unknown tongue occurs when the Spirit of God gives to man a heavenly language to communicate more effectively and efficiently to God in prayer. It is an unknown tongue (language) because it is not an earthly language known to men. The scripture says that no man (including the one speaking) understands him. This is why we say it is not the same as diverse tongues that can be understood by men. Hence it is appropriate to call it unknown tongues as added in italics by the translators and writers of the King James Version of the bible.

For he that speaketh in an *unknown* tongue speaketh not unto men, but unto God: for no man understandeth him; howbeit in the spirit he speaketh mysteries.

1 Corinthians 14:2

It is like having a direct phone line to God that cannot be interrupted or tapped into by any being or creature. We speak mysteries (the hidden wisdom of God) whenever we speak in unknown tongues.

Likewise the Spirit also helpeth our infirmities: for we know not what we should pray for as we ought: but the Spirit itself maketh intercession for us with groanings which cannot be uttered.

And he that searcheth the hearts knowethwhat is the mind of the Spirit, because he maketh intercession for the saints according to the will of God.

Romans 8:26-27

The Spirit of God helps us in our human limitations. There are many occasions where we do not know or are unsure about the perfect will of God. Thus hindering our ability to pray effectively and accurately in line with God's will. This would reduce our efficiency in prayer; however, the Holy Ghost makes intercession for us in prayer. He uses word or sounds which cannot be uttered, but which we can give voice to through our mouths and vocal chords. Because the Father and the Holy Spirit are always in agreement, He knows what the Holy Spirit is praying, because He (the Holy Spirit) always prays for us according to the will of God.

Some benefits of the baptism of the Holy Spirit

1. The baptism enables the believer to walk in God's power and manifest the evidence of Christ in the earth.

But ye shall receive power, after that the Holy Ghost is come upon you: and ye shall be witnesses unto me both in Jerusalem, and in all Judaea, and in Samaria, and unto the uttermost part of the earth.

Acts 1:8

The word "Power" is translated from the Greek word "Dunamis". The meaning of this word is as follows: a force, miraculous power, ability, abundance, meaning, might, strength and wonderful works.

The word "witness" is translated from the Greek word "Martus". It means a witness as in a judicial case. "Marturia" is the Greek word for evidence, record, report and testimony.

A "Martus" is a carrier of "Maturia". Therefore the believer who has been baptized in the Holy Ghost should therefore be a carrier of the evidence of both the Kingdom of God and of the Holy Ghost who dwells in him. This will happen when miracles, signs and wonders are made manifest through this type of believer. This means the believer who has being baptized with the Holy Ghost is enabled by God to carry and manifest the evidence of the Kingdom of God by signs and wonders produced through the help of the Holy Ghost.

Then Philip went down to the city of Samaria, and preached Christ unto them.
And <u>the people with one accord gave heed unto those things which Philip spake, hearing and seeing the miracles which he did</u>.
For unclean spirits, crying with loud voice, came out of many that were possessed with them: and many taken with palsies, and that were lame, were healed.

And there was great joy in that city.

Acts 8:5-8

2. This baptism allows the Holy Spirit to intercede on our behalf. One of the signs or evidence of the baptism of the Holy Ghost in the life of a born-again believer is the speaking with new tongues. "Tongues" means languages.

And these signs shall follow them that believe; In my name shall they cast out devils; they shall speak with new tongues; Mark 16:17

This is an unknown tongue as seen in 1 Corinthians 14:2. It is an entirely different experience from divers' tongues as seen in 1 Corinthians 12:10, which will be explained under the topic Gifts of the Holy Spirit. This tongue (language) is a heavenly language. 1 Corinthians 13:1 tells us it is possible to speak or pray (talking of prayer in the context of scripture) in the tongues of men or angels (heavenly language). Hence praying in unknown tongues is the Spirit of God giving to man a heavenly language to communicate more effectively and efficiently to God in prayer.

For he that speaketh in an unknown tongue speaketh not unto men, but unto God: for no man understandeth him; howbeit in the spirit he speaketh mysteries.
1 Corinthians 14:2

The scripture says that no man (including the person speaking in tongues) understands the manner of speech proceeding from the one speaking. This is why we say it is not the same as divers' tongues that can be understood by men. Hence, it is appropriate to call it unknown tongues as added in italics by the translators. It is like having a direct phone line to God that cannot be interrupted or bugged by anyone. We speak mysteries (the hidden wisdom of God) whenever we speak in unknown tongues.

Likewise the Spirit also helpeth our infirmities: for we know not what we should pray for as we ought: but the Spirit itself maketh intercession for us with groanings which cannot be uttered.
And he that searcheth the hearts knowethwhat is the mind of the Spirit, because he maketh intercession for the saints according to the will of God.
Romans 8:26-27

The Spirit of God helps us in our human limitations. Many a times we do not know what the perfect will of God is concerning any given situation. This in turn hinders our ability to pray effectively and accurately in line with God's will. However, the Holy Ghost makes intercession for us in prayer, using words or sounds that cannot be uttered, but which we can give voice to through our mouths and vocal chords. Because the Father and the Holy Spirit agree in all things, God knows and responds to that which the Holy Spirit is praying for us because He always prays according to the will of God.

3. You build/charge up your spirit man whenever you pray in the Holy Ghost.
There are many demands and challenges that the believer faces on a daily basis. These coupled with the fact that we are daily engaged in spiritual warfare, can leave the believer weary and depleted of strength in the inner man/spirit man. The Holy Ghost is the one we must rely on daily for strengthening of our inner man/spirit man.

For this cause I bow my knees unto the Father of our Lord Jesus Christ, Of whom the whole family in heaven and earth is named, That he would grant you, according to the riches of his glory, to be strengthened with might by his Spirit in the inner man;

Ephesians 3:14-16

Whenever we pray with the Holy Ghost there is a release of the strength of God (Zoe-the life of God) into our spirit man. This life of God strengthens our spirit man, pours out like a river from the abundance in our spirit man and edifies our soul, and rejuvenates (and repairs) our human bodies. This experience is both refreshing and restorative to our spirit, soul, and body, even as it endues and renews us with the strength of God in our spirit, soul, and body.

But ye, beloved, building up yourselves on your most holy faith, praying in the Holy Ghost

Jude Verse 20

In the last day, that great day of the feast, Jesus stood and cried, saying, If any man thirst, let him come unto me, and drink.
He that believeth on me, as the scripture hath said, out of his belly shall flow rivers of living water.
(But this spake he of the Spirit, which they that believe on him should receive: for the Holy Ghost was not yet given; because that Jesus was not yet glorified.)

John 8:37-39

But there is a spirit in man: and <u>the inspiration of the Almighty giveth them understanding.</u>

Job 32:8

But if the Spirit of him that raised up Jesus from the dead dwell in you, he that raised up Christ from the dead shall also <u>quicken your mortal</u> bodies by his Spirit that dwelleth in you.

Romans 8:11

How to be baptised in the Holy Ghost

There are certain guiding steps that can be used to get oneself or another person baptized in the Holy Ghost. Meditating upon these steps and the scriptures from the Bible given to back them coupled with simple child like faith in doing them would doubtless cause one to walk with God to experience the baptism of the Holy Ghost in the life of a born again believer.

There are specific instances where like the baptism of the Holy Spirit experience that took place at Cornelius home (Acts 8) where the Holy Spirit may move differently in speed and sovereignty to get people baptized. Such experiences are categorized as unique experiences and not the norm. Hence in this chapter we are preparing the students for the normal methodology which can be used by an individual to get baptized in the Holy Spirit either when alone or when ministered to by another party. These steps are guaranteed to work.

The steps are:

1. One must be born again in Christ Jesus. Ensure the person (or you) has accepted Jesus Christ as his/her Lord and Saviour in accordance to Romans 10:9-13. The Holy Spirit will not dwell in a human spirit which is not yet born again into the righteousness of God (2 Corinthians 6:14-18).

Who, when they were come down, prayed for them, that they might receive the Holy Ghost:
(For as yet he was fallen upon none of them: only they were baptized in the name of the Lord Jesus.)
Then laid they their hands on them, and they received the Holy Ghost.

Acts 8:15-17

2. One must desire to be baptised in the Holy Ghost. Ensure that the person truly desires to be baptized in the Holy Ghost. He/she must not be forced. It must be a free will choice born out of hunger and thirst for more of God.

In the last day, that great day of the feast, Jesus stood and cried, saying, If any man thirst, let him come unto me, and drink.
He that believeth on me, as the scripture hath said, out of his belly shall flow rivers of living water.
(But this spake he of the Spirit, which they that believe on him should receive: for the Holy Ghost was not yet given; because that Jesus was not yet glorified.)

John 7:37-39

Blessed are they which do hunger and thirst after righteousness: for they shall be filled.

Matthew 5:6

3. Ensure that there is no sin in your life. Sin when present in the life of a believer can sometimes hinder their faith to receive from God (though God is willing to give). This is because the person may feel condemned when standing before God in prayer, and may believe that God will not answer his/her prayer. This way, sin many times short circuits the flow of the power of God in a believer's life because of its negative influence on the believer's faith.

And their sins and iniquities will I remember no more.
Now where remission of these is, there is no more offering for sin.
Having therefore, brethren, boldness to enter into the holiest by the blood of Jesus,
By a new and living way, which he hath consecrated for us, through the veil, that is to say, his flesh;

And having an high priest over the house of God;
Let us draw near with a true heart in full assurance of faith, having our hearts sprinkled from an evil conscience, and our bodies washed with pure water.
Let us hold fast the profession of our faith without wavering; (for he is faithful that promised;)

Hebrews 10:17-23

For we have not an high priest which cannot be touched with the feeling of our infirmities; but was in all points tempted like as we are, yet without sin.
Let us therefore come boldly unto the throne of grace, that we may obtain mercy, and find grace to help in time of need.

Hebrews 4:15-16

Therefore, ask the person whether his/her lifestyle is right. Whatever response he/she gives, you must always ascertain this fact with the help of the Holy Ghost. The Holy Ghost will work with you throughout this process. If they are in sin, request them to ask God for forgiveness. Inform them of the importance of living right even after they are filled, as this would help to further build their intimacy with and faith in God, and thereby enhance their walk with the Holy Ghost.

Ye ask, and receive not, because ye ask amiss, that ye may consume it upon your lusts.

James 4:3

And when Simon saw that through laying on of the apostles' hands the Holy Ghost was given, he offered them money,
Saying, Give me also this power, that on whomsoever I lay hands, he may receive the Holy Ghost.
But Peter said unto him, Thy money perish with thee, because thou hast thought that the gift of God may be purchased with money.
Thou hast neither part nor lot in this matter: for thy heart is not right in the sight of God.
Repent therefore of this thy wickedness, and pray God, if perhaps the thought of thine heart may be forgiven thee.
For I perceive that thou art in the gall of bitterness, and in the bond of iniquity.
Then answered Simon, and said, Pray ye to the Lord for me, that none of these things which ye have spoken come upon me.

Acts 8:18-24

4. Build the persons faith to receive. It takes faith to receive the baptism of the Holy Spirit as the answer to Galatians 3:2, :5, & :14 indicates.

This only would I learn of you, Received ye the Spirit by the works of the law, or by the hearing of faith?
He therefore that ministereth to you the Spirit, and worketh miracles among you, doeth he it by the works of the law, or by the hearing of faith?

That the blessing of Abraham might come on the Gentiles through Jesus Christ; that <u>we might receive the promise of the Spirit through faith</u>.

Galatians 3:2, :5, & :14

Faith is a vital ingredient to receiving the baptism of the Holy Spirit. This faith is built into the recipient as he/she comes to hear and know what the scriptures rightly say about the baptism of the Holy Spirit (Romans 10:17). There is an impartation of spiritual understanding into the mind of the recipient, which helps to bring down strongholds (2 Corinthians 10:4-5) in the recipient's mind, and which may have caused fear or doubt in the mind of the recipient. This fear or doubts is the greatest hindrance in the mind of the recipient to the receiving by faith of the Holy Spirit baptism.

This is a continuous process that must be applied to ensure that at all times during the baptism there is no stumbling block of fear or doubt towards the whole process.

5. Ask from God in prayer. Lead the person in a prayer to ask for the baptism (infilling) of the Holy Ghost. We must not be afraid knowing that we are asking from our loving Heavenly Father. He not only hears us and grants our request in accordance with His word, but also would not allow us to receive a wrong or evil spirit when we ask of Him for His Holy Spirit.

And I say unto you, Ask, and it shall be given you; seek, and ye shall find; knock, and it shall be opened unto you. For every one that askethreceiveth; and he that seekethfindeth; and to him that knocketh it shall be opened. If a son shall ask bread of any of you that is a father, will he give him a stone? or if he ask a fish, will he for a fish give him a serpent? Or if he shall ask an egg, will he offer him a scorpion? If ye then, being evil, know how to give good gifts unto your children: how much more shall your heavenly Father give the Holy Spirit to them that ask him?

Luke 11:9-13

This is God's word to us assuring us of His nature and goodness (attributes) towards us. It is on this basis that we know that He will not only hear our prayer but that He will also not give us that which will hurt us.

6. Laying of hands in faith. If praying for someone else to get baptized in the Holy Ghost then you can join your faith to theirs by laying your hands on them as Apostles Peter and John did in Acts 8:17 and Apostle Paul did in Acts 19:6.

Who, when they were come down, prayed for them, that they might receive the Holy Ghost:
(For as yet he was fallen upon none of them: only they were baptized in the name of the Lord Jesus.)
<u>Then laid they their hands on them, and they received the Holy Ghost.</u>
<u>And when Simon saw that through laying on of the apostles' hands the Holy Ghost was given,</u> he offered them money,

Acts 8:15-18

And when Paul had laid his hands upon them, the Holy Ghost came on them; and they spake with tongues, and prophesied.

Acts 19:6

These are two instances in the Bible where people received the baptism of the Holy Ghost by the laying of hands of someone else who was already baptized in the Holy Ghost.

You do not have to hit the person hard with your hands, etc. It is not you baptizing them, it is the Holy Ghost. He knows what to do to make them filled with the Holy Ghost. You don't have to squeeze their throats or any such funny things. Yet there may be times when the Holy Ghost may lead you in some actions by His unction (leadings and promptings), but don't make a general doctrine out of such unique leadings. Do it in all righteousness and He will back it.

Then he answered and spake unto me, saying, This is the word of the Lord unto Zerubbabel, saying, Not by might, nor by power, but by my spirit, saith the Lord of hosts.

Zechariah 4:6-7

7. Open your mouth in faith and speak. Now assure the person that they are already filled and baptized with the Holy Ghost according to God's word in Luke 11:9-13.

Remember that as believers we are not to walk or receive by sight but by faith (2 Corinthians 5:7). Therefore, we should not look for, nor wait for an outward feeling or sign to confirm we are filled with the Holy Ghost. We are to believe that based on God's word, love and promise we are already filled because God cannot lie and He cannot fail. He loves us and will not withhold any good from us including the Holy Ghost (Proverbs 3:27).

Having known and understood that they are already filled with the Holy Ghost encourage them to speak out whatever the Holy Ghost puts in their vocal chords and mouth as in Acts 2:4. At the same time reminding them that what they would utter would not sound like a normal earthly language as in 1 Corinthians 14:2.

And they were all filled with the Holy Ghost, and began to speak with other tongues, as the Spirit gave them utterance.

Acts 2:4

Note that the disciples were first filled with the Holy Ghost, and then they began to speak afterwards. The Holy Spirit gave the utterance but they did the speaking. It is you that would open your mouth and speak (voice out) that which the Holy Ghost puts in your vocal chords.

8. Keep speaking and don't doubt what you have received. Speaking in unknown tongues for the first time is like a baby learning to speak a new language. Only this time it is a spiritual or heavenly language and as such even your mind will not understand what you are saying whenever you are speaking in unknown tongues. This is in harmony with what the word tells us in 1 Corinthians 14:2, except God gives you the grace to interpret what you said in unknown tongues.

i) Sometimes some people want to stop speaking in these unknown tongues because they do not understand what they are saying and it sounds gibberish. Yet you must remember and understand that this is both a spiritual and a heavenly language and as such it does not follow the rules of natural language. Even two different earthly languages can sometimes seem so different in rules from each other both in speech and in writing, how much more a language that is from heaven above in comparison with a language from the earth.

For my thoughts are not your thoughts, neither are your ways my ways, saith the Lord.
For as the heavens are higher than the earth, so are my ways higher than your ways, and my thoughts than your thoughts.
Isaiah 55:8-9

We should be encouraged to keep speaking in these unknown tongues knowing that our mind may be unfruitful, but our spirit by the help of the Holy Spirit is making meaningful intercession.

For if I pray in an unknown tongue, my spirit prayeth, but my understanding is unfruitful.
1 Corinthians 14:14

ii) The devil also recognizes that your ability to pray in unknown tongues will have disastrous impact on his kingdom and works, because of its accuracy in prayer and the power of God it generates, and as a result he will also seek to stop you from using this new weapon. This he will do by trying to make you doubt that you are not really speaking in unknown tongues. He cannot stop your mouth from speaking because this is not in his power, but he will try to send opposing and contradicting thoughts to your mind so as to convince you to use your own strength to stop praying in unknown tongues. He may even try to use external forces, such as other people in your life, to try convince you that what you are speaking is gibberish.

Likewise the Spirit also helpeth our infirmities: for we know not what we should pray for as we ought: but the Spirit itself maketh intercession for us with groanings which cannot be uttered.
And he that searcheth the hearts knowethwhat is the mind of the Spirit, because he maketh intercession for the saints according to the will of God.
Romans 8:26-27

We should be fully persuaded in ourselves about the truth and proper interpretation of the scriptures, knowing that the strange groaning or sounds we are making is not rubbish but the Holy Spirit praying according to the mind and will of God for us.

TEST YOURSELF
CHAPTER 11 – THE BAPTISM OF THE HOLY SPIRIT

The answer sheet is provided at the back of this manual.

1. Which of the following statements about the Holy Spirit is not true?

    a) The Holy Spirit comes to dwell in a person immediately after he/she becomes born again.
    b) There are numerous instances in scriptures where people got baptised with the Holy Ghost and then saved later.
    c) Jesus spoke of the experience of baptism of the Holy spirit as an infilling of the Holy Ghost.
    d) One of the evidence of the baptism of the Holy Ghost in the life of a believer is speaking with new tongues.

2. Praying in tongues can be described in all of the following ways except?

    a) It is a heavenly language.
    b) It is an experience of praying in unknown tongue.
    c) It is a language.
    d) It is part of the human languages.

3. Which one of the following is a benefit of baptism of the Holy Spirit?

    a) It causes us to become spiritually funny people.
    b) It enables us to live in God's power and manifest Christ wherever we are.
    c) It makes us viable to become church leaders.
    d) It causes us to speak in strange languages that we are not sure of.

4. The Holy Spirit comes to help us in our _____ because there are situations where we may not know or be unsure of the will of God.

5. It takes _____ to receive the baptism of the Holy Spirit as the answer to Galatians 3:2 and Galatians 3:5 indicate.

CHAPTER 12:
WORSHIP AND PRAISE

Worship

Now that we have been made priests unto our God, it becomes our duty to fellowship with God via the study of God's word, righteousness, worship, praise, prayer, walking in God's love etc. These acts of worship will facilitate our continuous fellowship and connection to God and ensure constant fruitfulness in God's kingdom and purposes for our life.

Then saith Jesus unto him, Get thee hence, Satan: for it is written, Thou shalt <u>worship the Lord thy God</u>, and him only shalt thou serve.

Matthew 4:10

What is worship?

The term worship brings many pictures to mind. To some it portrays slow songs, to others a holy reverence while to others it makes reference to prayer. What is the definition of worship? Worship is a term derived from two words: "worth" and "ship" or more plainly "worth-ship". It connotes the aspect of the worth of something or someone. It is a reverential term giving value to a person, a thing, etc.E.g. His worship the mayor.

In our context, the highest worship is ascribed unto God for He declared that He alone is God and there is no other beside Him.

We can therefore define worship as our willful expression of God's worth or value due to Him, or giving God His due worth.

Worship therefore translates into whatever we do or engage ourselves in that shows or gives God His value in our lives. It is our expression of God's worth or value due to Him. This may be expressed from our heart; through our lifestyle, our obedience to God, our walking in righteousness, songs of praise, giving of tithes and offerings, etc.

Worship as a lifestyle

Worship therefore, can be offered to God twenty-four (24) hours of the day, because even our eating, sleeping, playing, etc, should be done in worship (obedience) to God. Whatever we do, we are to do it in reverence to God and in seeking to please Him. Hence, worship ceases to be an occasion or event but becomes our lifestyle.

This disqualifies the notion that worship is the singing of a slow song, since God's worth cannot be limited to singing only.

I beseech you therefore, brethren, by the mercies of God, that ye present your bodies a living sacrifice, holy, acceptable unto God, which is your reasonable service.

Romans 12:1

So, brothers, with God's tender feelings, I beg you to offer your bodies as a living, holy, pleasing sacrifice to God. This is <u>true worship from you</u>.

Romans 12:1 (Simple English translation)

Worship God with all you are and have

Worship can be expressed through a variety of methods. Whatever method of worship we use we should worship God with our spirit, our soul, our body, and our strengths. The scripture states that our **spirit**, **soul**, **body** and **all our strengths** should be used to express worship to God at all times.

And Jesus answered him, The first of all the commandments is, Hear, O Israel; The Lord our God is one Lord:
And thou shalt love the Lord thy God with <u>all thy heart</u>, and with <u>all thy soul, and with all thy mind</u>, and with <u>all thy strength</u>: this is the first commandment.

Mark 12:29-30

Our spirit, our soul, and our body encompass everything that we are and everything that we have. Therefore, the wholeness of who we are should be used to worship God every second of everyday of our lives.

Hear, O Israel: the Lord our God is one Lord:
And thou shalt love the Lord thy God with all <u>thine heart</u> *(spiritman)*, and with all <u>thy soul</u>, and with all <u>thy might</u> *(body-physical strength)*.

Deuteronomy 6:4-5

Our strengths include all the other resources outside of our being that are at our disposal and useful to us for living. Examples of such strengths include our relationships, influence, wealth, talents, gifts, etc. We should remember that there is nothing in our possession or at our disposal that has not been given to us by God. In other words, we are not the creators of anything inherent in us or available to us. All that we have came from God. Due to this truth, we should use our resources or resources available to us to worship God and bring glory to Him always. This is further emphasized in the scriptures below.

Honour the LORD with thy substance, and with the firstfruits of all thine increase:

Proverbs 3:9

Praise

Praise forms the second half of a subject that has been very confusing for many people, i.e. praise and worship. The two subjects (praise and worship), have for a long time and in many parts of the Church been mistaken to deal with fast and slow songs respectively. This has for a long time given the impression that whenever believers assemble and participate in singing some fast and slow songs that they have praised (erroneously thought to be the fast song) and worshiped (erroneously thought to be the slow song). As we found out on the subject of worship, this notion is far from the truth. We will find out in this section that this concept of praise is also far from the truth.

What is Praise?

Praise can be defined as the act(s) of thanking, proclaiming, exalting, and glorifying God. It is also an act or a form of worship, but not the only mode of worship.

By him therefore let us offer the sacrifice of praise to God continually, that is, the fruit of our lips giving thanks to his name.
Hebrews 13:15

Praise is a sacrifice we offer onto God. Praise embraces an attitude of gratitude to God at all times and in all things whether good or bad. That means praise becomes the unconditional attitude of the believer in His response to God and the issues of life. As a result, we should seek every opportunity to attribute praise to God. Every good and every perfect situation is attributed chiefly to the goodness of God.

Although the fig tree shall not blossom, neither shall fruit be in the vines; the labour of the olive shall fail, and the fields shall yield no meat; the flock shall be cut off from the fold, and there shall be no herd in the stalls:
Yet I will rejoice in the Lord, I will joy in the God of my salvation.
Habakkuk 3:17-18

I will bless the Lord at all times: his praise shall continually be in my mouth.
Psalms 34:1

Praise from a heart of worship

Praise must be offered from a heart of worship towards God. If one does not worship God (lifestyle), then his/her praise will not be effective. Worship (the lifestyle) gives strength to praise. It is a lifestyle of worship that generates the power behind praise. Therefore, praise is not complete without a lifestyle of worship.

This should explain why a person with a pleasant voice can lead a congregation in singing songs of praise to God yet fail "to draw in the presence of God". On the other hand, we can encounter the converse, where one with a somewhat croaky voice can effectively "draw into the gathering" the presence of God. It has been observed that these differences in ability to usher into a gathering the presence of God is caused by the variance in the lifestyle of worship. It can be authoritatively concluded that the person with a stronger lifestyle of worship (whether fine or croaky voice) will be more effective in drawing in the presence of God. We are not advocating for a lack of skillfulness in music with these observations, rather we are emphasizing the importance of a lifestyle of worship towards God.

Therefore, the strength of praise is not in the sound of our voice but in the daily lifestyle of worship behind the voice. This will definitely lead to a continuous manifestation of the presence of God in the praises of that worshipper. A person who departs from such a lifestyle would soon experience a decrease in the tangibility of the manifestation of God's presence during praise.

Methods of praise

Praise can be expressed through a variety of ways, such as: Through our lips by speaking, singing (or humming a melody), making a joyful noise (shouting, or making sounds with our mouth), and by speaking or singing with the Spirit.

I will bless the Lord at all times: his praise shall continually be in my mouth.
Psalm 34:1

I will be glad and rejoice in thee: I will sing praise to thy name, O thou most High.
Psalm 9:2

O Clap your hands, all ye people; <u>shout unto God</u> with the voice of triumph.
Psalm 47:1

What is it then? I will pray with the spirit, and I will pray with the understanding also<u>: I will sing with the spirit</u> (in unknown tongues)**, and I will sing with the understanding also.**
1 Corinthians 14:15

Praise can also be expressed through our human body by clapping our hands, dancing (any type of body movement-bowing, jumping, twisting, etc), and the playing of musical instruments. The methods of praise cannot be exhausted, because the Spirit of God can always lead us into new ways of praising God.

Praise him with the timbrel and dance:…..
Psalm 150:4a

O come, let us worship and bow down: let us kneel before the Lord our maker.
Psalm 95:6

Thus will I bless thee while I live: I will lift up my hands in thy name.

Psalm 63:4

Praise can be very dynamic and wholesome when we involve our spirit, our soul (involving your intellect, imagination, memory, emotions, and will) and our body. It also becomes more fulfilling and real to the one offering it to God.

All these different methods of expressions of praise are acceptable with God as long as they are done in worship unto God and not for showing off. It is not a performance unto men but unto God. God must remain the single audience to whom we are performing, or seeking to please.

Purposes of praise

Apart from the use of praise to express our gratitude to God and to worship God, praise also has other purposes. Some of the other purposes of praise are:

1.Praise helps in building intimacy with God. Praise is an act of fellowship that builds intimacy between God and man. It ushers one into the manifestation of God's presence.

But thou art holy, O thou that inhabitest the praises of Israel *(other translations – your people)*.

Psalms 22:3

God inhabits the praises of His people, therefore, God and His people are made one in praise. It is within praise that God and the saint cohabit.

Enter into his gates with thanksgiving, and into his courts with praise: be thankful unto him, and bless his name.

Psalm 100:4

2. Praise is a weapon of war that evokes God to wage war on our behalf. God can be evoked through praise into waging war against the saints' enemies. These enemies include both spiritual and physical principalities, who are opposed to the advancement of God's Kingdom and His saints.

Let the high praises of God be in their mouth, And a two-edged sword in their hand,
To execute vengeance on the nations, And punishments on the peoples;
To bind their kings with chains, And their nobles with fetters of iron;
To execute on them the written judgment This honor have all His saints. Praise the Lord!

Psalm 149:6-9

But at midnight Paul and Silas were praying and singing hymns to God, and the prisoners were listening to them.

Suddenly there was a great earthquake, so that the foundations of the prison were shaken; and immediately all the doors were opened and everyone's chains were loosed.

Acts 16:25-26

An earlier quoted scripture clearly showed to us that God inhabits the praises of his people (Psalm 22:3). This means that where there is true and righteous praises offered to God, He is always present. His presence makes His enemies to scatter and their strength to melt like wax in the presence of fire. God wages war on the behalf of His saints by simply showing up.

Let God arise, Let His enemies be scattered; Let those also who hate Him flee before Him.
As smoke is driven away, So drive them away; As wax melts before the fire, So let the wicked perish at the presence of God.

Psalm 68:1-2

Therefore, one should sing songs of praise, which are consistent with the manifestation of God we want to see. This is important because the songs sang, will evoke God according to the proclamation or declaration in them. For example, we sing songs that praise God as a healer, when we want or desire to evoke His healing attributes in our midst.

3. Praise activates the hand and blessings of God in one's favour. Praise causes us to walk in the favour and blessings of God. A lifestyle of praising God and always showing appreciation will bring us into a place of fruitfulness in the blessings of God. This will occur to a point where the inhabitants of the earth will be awed and fear God.

Let the people praise thee, O God; let all the people praise thee.
Then shall the earth yield her increase; and God, even our own God, shall bless us.
God shall bless us; and all the ends of the earth shall fear him.

Psalm 67:5-7

When we praise God and He inhabits our praises, He comes with His goodness, mercies, and grace. Therefore praising God causes the goodness, the mercies, and the presence of God, to be attracted to us, watering us like a cloud from heaven. This causes the seeds of God's word that we have planted in our hearts, to bring forth fruit. It is one of the Kingdom principles which the saint must discipline themselves to walk in, if we want to see our lives, families, churches, businesses, organizations, etc, come into fruitfulness.

Sing, O barren, thou that didst not bear; break forth into singing, and cry aloud, thou that didst not travail with child: for more are the children of the desolate than the children of the married wife, saith the Lord.

Enlarge the place of thy tent, and let them stretch forth the curtains of thine habitations: spare not, lengthen thy cords, and strengthen thy stakes;
For thou shalt break forth on the right hand and on the left; and thy seed shall inherit the Gentiles, and make the desolate cities to be inhabited.

Isaiah 54:1-3

TEST YOURSELF
CHAPTER 12 – WORSHIP AND PRAISE

The answer sheet is provided at the back of this manual.

1. Which of the following statements about praise is not true?

    a) It serves to help build intimacy with God.
    b) It is the only mode of worship that evokes God to act on our behalf.
    c) Activates the hand and blessings of God on our favour.
    d) Evokes God to act on our behalf.

2. Worship can be defined in all of the following ways except:

    a) The aspect of the worth of something or someone.
    b) Worship translates into whatever we do or engage ourselves in that gives God His value in our lives.
    c) It is our expression of God's worth or value due to Him.
    d) It portrays only singing slow songs.

3. Which of the following is true about the purpose of praise?

    a) It helps to build our intimacy with God.
    b) It is a strategy to help us lose weight through dancing.
    c) The faster the praise song the better the mood.
    d) It is what we do to prepare us to worship God in spirit and in truth.

4. Praise must be offered from a _____ towards God.

5. Praise can be very _____ and wholesome when we involve our spirit, our soul and our body.

CHAPTER 13:

PRAYER

As a priest of the Most High God, the believer must know how to commune with God through prayer. Prayer is one of the many sacrifices that this priest must learn to offer onto God both effectively and fervently.

What is prayer?

Prayer is the art of communication between a believer and God. It is man communing with God. Prayer therefore is simply communicating with God.

As with communication, there are two parties; the caller and the receiver, who are both actively involved in exchange of information. Likewise, we find that prayer is the place of both parties exchanging information through a heart to heart communication. This clearly implies that communication is two-way in its nature. Owing to the fact that prayer is communication, this definition therefore affirms that prayer is a dialogue and not a monologue as it has degenerated to, in many circles. This can be seen in the way Abraham communed with God when God told Him of His plan to destroy Sodom and Gomorrah. There was a two-way dialogue taking place between God and Abraham.

And the men turned their faces from thence, and went toward Sodom: but Abraham stood yet before the Lord.
And Abraham drew near, and said, Wilt thou also destroy the righteous with the wicked?
Peradventure there be fifty righteous within the city: wilt thou also destroy and not spare the place for the fifty righteous that are therein?
That be far from thee to do after this manner, to slay the righteous with the wicked: and that the righteous should be as the wicked, that be far from thee: shall not the Judge of all the earth do right?
And the Lord said, If I find in Sodom fifty righteous within the city, then I will spare all the place for their sakes.
And Abraham answered and said, Behold now, I have taken upon me to speak unto the Lord, which am but dust and ashes:
Peradventure there shall lack five of the fifty righteous: wilt thou destroy all the city for lack of five? And he said, If I find there forty and five, I will not destroy it.
And he spake unto him yet again, and said, Peradventure there shall be forty found there. And **he said**, I will not do it for forty's sake.

And <u>he said unto him</u>, Oh let not the Lord be angry, and I will speak: Peradventure there shall thirty be found there. And <u>he said</u>, I will not do it, if I find thirty there.
And <u>he said</u>, Behold now, I have taken upon me to speak unto the Lord: Peradventure there shall be twenty found there. <u>And he said</u>, I will not destroy it for twenty's sake.
And <u>he said</u>, Oh let not the Lord be angry, and I will speak yet but this once: Peradventure ten shall be found there. And <u>he said</u>, I will not destroy it for ten's sake.
And the Lord went his way, as soon as <u>he had left communing with Abraham</u>: and Abraham returned unto his place.

Genesis 18:22-33

Why we pray

Three primary purposes of prayer are:

1. For fellowship with God. This ought to be like when one talks to a friend for the purposes of building intimacy and enjoying each others' company. Prayer is one of the links for fellowship between God and man, and therefore it is instrumental in the strengthening of the relationship between God and man. Men like Moses developed such intimate fellowship with God even in their fallen state.

And the Lord spake unto Moses face to face, as a man speaketh unto his friend. And he turned again into the camp: but his servant Joshua, the son of Nun, a young man, departed not out of the tabernacle.

Exodus 33:11

This fellowship should not be characterized by religious clichés and an endless list of petitions, but by friendship.

Draw near to God and He will draw near to you. Cleanse your hands, you sinners; and purify your hearts, you double-minded.

James 4:8

In the above-cited scripture, the Apostle James exhorts us to draw near to God that He may draw near to us. This scripture can also be rendered as, "the manner or the fashion with which we approach God determines how He relates to us". It must be remembered that fellowship is for friends and not for servants. We are called to be friends of God, and yes, friends who also serve in His great Kingdom (John 15:14-15).

2. For personal edification. It is as the saint develops intimate fellowship with God that he/she accesses divine edification. Every time the believer connects with God in prayer, divine power and strength flows inwards from God to the believer, charging the believer with the divine life (Zoe) of God. The believer then becomes a carrier of God's divine life, regenerating every area of his/her being. It charges or replenishes him/her with

God-given strength of character, pureness, righteousness, wisdom, power, etc. It is like when two friends spend time fellowshipping together, they end up rubbing off on each other. In this case, it is God's divine life and presence that rubs on to the one spending time in communication with Him. Therefore when we pray, we make power available like charging a battery.

But ye, beloved, building up yourselves on your most holy faith, praying in the Holy Ghost,

Jude Verse 20

In Jude verse 20, the word edification also means to charge or build up. "Charging" here refers to the use of the word as used in the re-powering of a car battery that has been drained. This impartation results in the spiritual muscles of the saint being strengthened for more explorations in faith, the gifts/purposes of God within the believer are stirred up to a new dimension, and the saints are strengthened to radiate the glory of God on the earth. This is demonstrated during the earthly ministry of Jesus, when He went to pray on a mountain. God allowed the disciples who went up with Him to see the result of a prayerful life, which had become radiant with the power of God as displayed in the transfiguration of Jesus.

And after six days Jesus taketh Peter, James, and John his brother, and bringeth them up into an high mountain apart,
And was transfigured before them: and his face did shine as the sun, and his raiment was white as the light.

Matthew 17:1-2

3. For invoking the hand and strength of God. To invoke means to appeal to, to call upon, to seek the intervention of, and to bring into play. To invoke God therefore implies to seek the intervention of God in order to enjoy His strength as pertains to any given issue or concern.

Call unto me, and I will answer thee, and shew thee great and mighty things, which thou knowest not.

Jeremiah 33:3

After building intimate fellowship with God through prayer, and being edified to a place of walking in the power of God, the believer can now easily invoke God. This is true because, having been edified by intimate fellowship with God, such a believer has built within him/herself a good grasp of the mind of Christ, hence the ability to know what to do to move the hand of God.

The drama that unfolded in the confrontation between Elijah and the prophets of Baal, shows the invocation of God by Elijah through prayer. Elijah displayed confidence in God, having full assurance that He (God) would respond as requested. His ability to invoke God (provoke the intervention of His hand) was also in Elijah's ministry, when He shut up and later opened the heaven through prayer.

Confess your faults one to another, and pray one for another, that ye may be healed. The effectual fervent prayer of a righteous man availeth much.
Elias was a man subject to like passions as we are, and he prayed earnestly that it might not rain: and it rained not on the earth by the space of three years and six months.
And he prayed again, and the heaven gave rain, and the earth brought forth her fruit.

James 5:16-18

How to pray

It is important for the believer to learn to pray skillfully in order to effectively communicate with God as a Priest. As shown in the scripture below, prayer can be taught.

And it came to pass, that, as he was praying in a certain place, when he ceased, one of his disciples said unto him, <u>Lord, teach us to pray</u>, as John also taught his disciples.
And <u>he said unto them</u>, When ye pray, say, ...

Luke 11:1-2(a)

Some guidelines to prayer are:

1. We are to direct our prayer to God. We are to direct our prayers to God the father. This is important because God the father sits as chief in the Godhead and is our father. Directing our prayers to Him therefore is in recognition of the order that exists in the Godhead and in acknowledgement of Him as our source. Jesus beautifully qualified this condition by categorically making it clear as shown in the scripture below.

So He said to them, "When you pray, say: Our Father in heaven, hallowed be Your name.

Luke 11:2(a)

"But you, when you pray, go into your room, and when you have shut your door, pray to your Father who is in the secret place; and your Father who sees in secret will reward you openly.

Matthew 6:6

We should also realise that we are communing with a living God and not an idol. Therefore He is real and can hear us.

Behold, the LORD'S hand is not shortened, that it cannot save; neither his ear heavy, that it cannot hear:

Isaiah 59:1

2. We should approach in the name of Jesus. This means when we pray to the Father we must pray using the name of Jesus. This of cause does not mean that we cannot speak words of fellowship to Jesus, yet all major requests should be directed to the Father.

And in that day ye shall ask me nothing. Verily, verily, I say unto you, <u>Whatsoever ye shall ask the Fatherin my name</u>, he will give it you.
Hitherto have ye asked nothing in my name: ask, and ye shall receive, that yourjoy may be full.

John 16:23-24

This condition can be logically explained when we consider the path to our redemption. This is because Jesus was the sacrificial lamb that was sacrificed to bring about our redemption. Jesus has become our mediator of this new covenant we have with God and He is now our High Priest. Without Him, our access to God ceases to be and we remain alienated from God. We are given access to God through Him, God sees us through Him.

Jesus saith unto him, I am the way, the truth, and the life: no man cometh unto the Father, but by me.

John 14:6

Therefore whenever we use the name of Jesus as we pray to the father, we are coming to the Father in the name (Person, Authority, and Power) of Jesus Christ.

3. Use the word of God skilfully to plead your case in harmony with God's will. God answers prayer that is in harmony with His will, because anything contrary to His will hinders His plans and purposes in the earth. This is why we should make sure that our requests are in line with God's will and the advancement of God's Kingdom in the earth. God's will and God's rightly divided (interpreted) word are one.

And this is the confidence that we have in him, that, if we ask any thing according to his will, he heareth us:
And if we know that he hear us, whatsoever we ask, we know that we have the petitions that we desired of him.

1 John 5:14-15

After this manner therefore pray ye: Our Father which art in heaven, Hallowed be thy name.
<u>Thy kingdom come. Thy will be done in earth, as it is in heaven</u>.

Matthew 6:9-10

Ye ask, and receive not, because ye ask amiss, that ye may consume it upon your lusts.

James 4:3

If God is the judge of all creation (Isaiah 33:22), then just like when standing before any judge who honours the law of the land we must also learn to use the word of God in our prayer sessions. God looks out for strong reasons why He should positively respond to one's petitions and requests. God is governed by the supremacy of His word (Psalm 138:2) and in it is found the predictability of God. We can tell how God will respond to any given situation because of what His word says concerning that given subject matter.

Come now, and let us reason together, saith the Lord: though your sins be as scarlet, they shall be as white as snow; though they be red like crimson, they shall be as wool.

Isaiah 1:18

4. Start and finish your prayer time with gratitude and appreciation to God. A prayer backed by gratitude (both in the beginning and in the end) is a prayer offered in faith. The gratitude and appreciation is a sign that one believes that whatever it is that they came into God's presence to do or request, has been heard and answered. This is an act of faith which shows that you believe God has heard your prayer request.

Enter into his gates with thanksgiving, and into his courts with praise: be thankful unto him, and bless his name.

Psalms 100:4

Be careful for nothing; but in every thing by prayer and supplication with thanksgiving let your requests be made known unto God.
And the peace of God, which passeth all understanding, shall keep your hearts and minds through Christ Jesus.

Philippians 4:6-7

Also by adding thanksgiving to prayer, one accesses the supernatural peace of God that surpasses human understanding, which gives him/her an assurance that God has heard and is responding to the petition.

5. Prayer must be backed by a lifestyle of righteousness. Communication is more than verbal. It would seem ridiculous if one was presented with a gift of great value and they received it with a frown on the face. It would not matter how deeply pleased and grateful they are concerning the gift, the frown on their face tells otherwise. In like fashion, we communicate to God in more than just verbal terms, and since prayer is communicating with God, we can then deduce that we pray even with our lifestyles. It is therefore correct to say that righteousness is a form of prayer, because it covers our lifestyle. The righteousness of the one praying therefore aids or hinders the effectiveness of his/her prayers.

Confess your faults one to another, and pray one for another, that ye may be healed. The effectual fervent prayer of a righteous man availeth much.

James 5:16

The text here does not refer to the prayer made in righteousness, but to the righteousness (both the righteous nature and the right lifestyle) of the man that is offering the prayer. The word "righteousness" as taught in this book finds application in all areas of life. Therefore, the manner in which we live our lives, whether at home, at work or in our leisure times, constitute part of our prayer. This largely explains why many are praying but only a few realize the full power of their prayers.

The Lord is far from the wicked: but he heareth the prayer of the righteous.

Proverbs 15:29

In many instances of prayer, the earlier considered steps on how to pray are never the problem but this one. We make many utterances that are accurate according the word of God, yet we live our lives in terms contrary to our speech. Because of this, prayer is short circuited and hence rendered ineffective.

When do we pray?

Saints are to pray to God whenever there is a need to pray, this may be during the day or even during the night, as long as there is a need to pray. Using our understanding of the purposes of prayer, there is a need to pray whenever there is a need to fellowship with God, edify yourself in God, or/and invoke God's hand.

Let us therefore come boldly unto the throne of grace, that we may obtain mercy, and find grace to help <u>in time of need</u>.

Hebrews 4:16

Jesus Christ never compromised whenever there was need for prayer (dialogue) with the Father. He would even stop His Kingly duties (i.e. establishing the Kingdom of God in the earth, and in the lives of men), in order to spend time in His Priestly ministry (fellowship with God in prayer).

**But so much the more went there a fame abroad of him: and great multitudes came together to hear, and to be healed by him of their infirmities.
And <u>he withdrew himself into the wilderness, and prayed</u>.**

Luke 5:15-16

We should learn to live a lifestyle of prayer. This is a lifestyle of continuous communication with God. It might be broken into short but frequent moments of speaking to and hearing from God, or it might be setting aside periods of time when and where we engage God in dialogue.

<u>Praying always</u> with all prayer and supplication in the Spirit, and watching thereunto with all perseverance and supplication for all saints;

Ephesians 6:18

Where do we pray?

The saint is the temple of God in this dispensation of grace and truth therefore s/he is the acceptable place of prayer. There is therefore no need for one to seek to travel to any Holy land, in order to offer sacrifices to God. We are to now worship God in spirit and in truth from God's holy temple (the born again believer) in this new dispensation.

Know ye not that ye are the temple of God, and that the Spirit of God dwelleth in you?

1 Corinthians 3:16

The woman saith unto him, Sir, I perceive that thou art a prophet.
Our fathers worshipped in this mountain; and ye say, that in Jerusalem is the place where men ought to worship.
Jesus saith unto her, Woman, believe me, the hour cometh, when ye shall neither in this mountain, nor yet at Jerusalem, worship the Father.
Ye worship ye know not what: we know what we worship: for salvation is of the Jews.
But the hour cometh, and now is, when the true worshippers shall worship the Father in spirit and in truth: for the Father seeketh such to worship him.
God is a Spirit: and they that worship him must worship him in spirit and in truth.

John 4:19-24

We are now His Holy place in the earth where God has chosen to put His name, and where prayer and worship is to be made to Him. We do not have to go to physical Israel for God to hear our prayers, He hears us wherever we are.

However, it is important that when we pray, we observe some ethical factors. One such example is to find a place (e.g. at home), where we will not be disturbed or distracted, and likewise we will not disturb others as we seek the face of our God.

And in the morning, rising up a great while before day, he went out, and departed into a solitary place, and there prayed.

Mark 1:35

TEST YOURSELF
CHAPTER 13 – PRAYER

The answer sheet is provided at the back of this manual.

1. As a priest unto God a believer must know how to commune with God through:

   a) Serving others in church.
   b) Prayer.
   c) Attending the church service early Sunday morning.
   d) Clapping their hands unto God.

2. Prayer can be defined in all of the following ways except:

   a) The art of communication between a believer and God through prayer.
   b) It is man communing with God.
   c) Prayer is simply communicating with God.
   d) Giving God his due.

3. Which one of the following describes the purposes of prayer?

   a) It is an avenue to express our complaints to God.
   b) It is an exercise we do to fulfill Christian obligation.
   c) It is an avenue to develop intimate fellowship with God.
   d) It is where we confess and possess what we want.

4. It is important that we learn that prayer must be backed by a lifestyle of _____.

5. A prayer backed by _____ is a prayer offered in faith.

CHAPTER 14:

LOVE

We as Christians are commanded by God to love all fellow believers, the unbelievers and even our enemies. Most important of all, we are to love the Lord God Almighty. Sometimes it can get pretty confusing and even lead to unnecessary hurts or burdens in our Christian walk if we do not first define what love is and then learn which type of love to appropriate to the different relationships we have on the earth.

In the scriptures the word "love" has different meanings because they are derived from a variety of words in the Hebrew and Greek languages. With the translation of the Testaments into the English language, the word love was used for all the different words used in the Hebrew and Greek manuscripts. Hence the importance of knowing which type of love is being spoken of in the diverse passages of the Bible.

Another reason why it is important to know the different types of love is because even in present day communication, the word love is used to describe different positions of relationships. For example, the word can be used in speech as follows, I love my Husband, I love my cat, I love food, and etc obviously the love a person has for her husband is not the same love they have for food.

The different types of love

The words used in the original manuscripts and later translated as the English word love are as follows.

1. Agape. This is a Greek word that expresses unconditional love. It is the love of God. It means a type of love that has no conditions attached to it. It has no conditions for loving you.

But God commendeth his love toward us, in that, while we were yet sinners, Christ died for us.

Romans 5:8

It is a love that is willing to help you be, to have, and to do everything God ordained you to be or have, and do, even if I don't know you. It wants you to enjoy and experience what it is enjoying and experiencing. Someone does not have to do something good to you or be your friend in order for you to agape them. God Himself had agape towards us even when we were yet His enemies. He is the greatest example of agape.

He that loveth not knoweth not God; for God is love.

1 John 4:8

This love is described in greater detail in 1 Corinthians 13:1-7 where it is also referred to as charity.

2. Phileo. This is a Greek word that expresses the kind of love between friends. It is a love of affiliation. It is the type of love where two people get along very well together. Phileo more nearly represents "tender affection". This is the kind of love we see between Jesus and John the disciple, and between David and Jonathan. Although in the Hebrew language it is called by another name.

Now there was leaning on Jesus' bosom one of his disciples, whom Jesus loved.

John 13:23

3. Storge. This is the love that exists in a family, though family members can also express agape and phileo to one another.Storge is the love that makes a person concerned about their family members.

4. Eros. This is the Latin word for Erotic or sensual love (sexual). It is from here that we derive the English word erotic. It is the love that should be exchanged only between a man and his wife. In the Hebrew language, the word used to express this kind of love is the Hebrew word "ahab" as used in Proverbs 5:19.

5. Combined words. Sometimes in the scriptures the different types of love are combined in meaning.

The practicality of walking in love.

All born again believers have been given the ability to walk in agape. This is because this love of God has been put into us by the Holy Spirit the minute we became children of God. Yet we will need to develop this potential on our inside and grow in it with time.

And hope maketh not ashamed; because the love of God is shed abroad in our hearts by the Holy Ghost which is given unto us.

Romans 5:5

But this does not necessarily imply that you should become best friends (sharing of phileo) with every believer in the church, or that you go to the house of him who wishes you harm. But you need to walk in agape towards all men (believers and unbelievers alike), wishing everyone well, and do whatever is in your power to help, lift up, or improve another person's life, while holding back nothing.

We should also keep agape as the foundation in every other type of relationship where we express the other types of love. This way agape will not allow the relationships to break and abort when the other types of love fail, because agape never fails or ceases.

Charity never faileth: but whether there be prophecies, they shall fail; whether there betongues, they shall cease; whether there be knowledge, it shall vanish away.

1 Corinthians 13:8

More on the practicality of the love of God is seen in 1 Corinthians 13:4-7.The practical principles by which agape work are recorded in the scriptures. We therefore come to understand agape not as an emotional feeling but as practical principles which we can engage in our everyday life.

Charity suffereth long, and is kind; charity envieth not; charity vaunteth not itself, is not puffed up,
Doth not behave itself unseemly, seeketh not her own, is not easily provoked, thinketh no evil;
Rejoiceth not in iniquity, but rejoiceth in the truth;
Beareth all things, believeth all things, hopeth all things, endureth all things.

1 Corinthians 13:4-7

We can examine the same scriptures from the Simple English version of the Bible in order to have a clear understanding of these principles or the practicality of agape.

A loving person is patient; is kind; is not jealous; is not boastful; is not proud; is not rude; is not interested only in himself; is even-tempered; does not hold grudges;
is not happy when someone else does wrong; is happy when truth wins;
never quits; always trusts; always hopes; always keeps on going.

1 Corinthians 13:4-7 (Simple English translation)

Love (agape) is a character which must be developed in every born again believer in Christ Jesus. It is part of the nature of God, because God is Love. The person who does not walk in the love (agape) of God is not considered spiritually mature in the Kingdom of God. To walk in love in all we do (E.g. when praying, when walking in the manifestations of the Holy Spirit, and when we give or serve in God's Kingdom) is to be said to be walking in God or in true Christ-like Kingdom maturity.

Beloved, let us love one another: for love is of God; and every one that loveth is born of God, and knoweth God.
He that loveth not knoweth not God; for God is love.

1 John 4:7-8

Though I speak with the tongues of men and of angels, and have not charity, I am become as sounding brass, or a tinkling cymbal.
And though I have the gift of prophecy, and understand all mysteries, and all

knowledge; and though I have all faith, so that I could remove mountains, and have not charity, I am nothing.
And though I bestow all my goods to feed the poor, and though I give my body to be burned, and have not charity, it profiteth me nothing.

1 Corinthians 13:1-3

We can also examine 1 Corinthians 13:1-3 from the Simple English version of the Bible in order to have a clearer understanding of God's perspective of the born again man/woman who does not walk in love (agape).

Even if I speak with human languages or the language of angels, but do not have loving concern, I have only become like the noisy sound of a gong or the ringing sound from cymbals.
I may have the ability to prophesy, know all secrets, possess all knowledge, and have the kind of faith which can move mountains, but if I don't have concern for others, I am nothing.
I could give away everything I own and sacrifice my body, so that I could brag about it, but if I did not have love, I have gained nothing.

1 Corinthians 13:1-3 (Simple English translation)

TEST YOURSELF
CHAPTER 14 – LOVE

The answer sheet is provided at the back of this manual.

1. Which of the following is not true about love?

   a) We are commanded by God to love all fellow believers.
   b) Most important of all we are to love the Lord God Almighty.
   c) In scripture the word love has many meanings.
   d) The love of God is the only type of love we have.

2. What is true about walking in love?

   a) All born again believers lack the ability to walk in agape.
   b) The love of God has been put in our hearts by our maturity.
   c) We need to walk in Agape towards all men.
   d) All of the above.

3. Which of the following is a type of love?

   a) Storge.
   b) Feeling.
   c) Emotions.
   d) Thoughts.

4. Agape is a type of love that _____.

5. _____is the love that should be exchanged only between a husband and his wife.

CHAPTER 15:
DIVINE RELATIONSHIPS

Relationships

Relationships basically talk of the position of a person(s) or thing towards another. They define the position of engagement between different people or things. For example, a father and a son relationship, meaning that one of the participants in the relationship is a father to the other, while the other is the son, etc. God has ordained man to be relational with the rest of God's creations in order for man to prosper in fulfilling God's purposes on the earth. We call these relationships that God has ordained for human beings; "divine relationships".

Any relationship ordained of God is designed to take one closer to God's designed destiny (destination of fullness of purpose) for one's life. Any relationship not ordained of God is set to influence one away from God's designed destiny. It is therefore important to discern, embrace, and only cultivate relationships that influence one towards God's designed destiny.

He that walketh with wise men shall be wise: but a companion of fools shall be destroyed.

Proverbs 13:20

Fellowship

This refers to the interaction that takes place within a relationship. It is fellowship that gives strength to relationship. A relationship without meaningful interaction or fellowship will not produce any fruit. These fruits are also called the benefits of that relationship. Fellowship talks of our working at making the relationship successful. Relationships are developed and maintained through proper relevant fellowship. Every type of relationship has its own type and boundaries of fellowship. E.g. a Christian man who is engaged to a Christian lady cannot have sex, yet a married man can have sex with his wife.

Rebuke not an elder, but intreat him as a father; and the younger men as brethren;
The elder women as mothers; the younger as sisters, with all purity.

1 Timothy 5:1-2

Iron sharpeneth iron; so a man sharpeneth the countenance of his friend.

Proverbs 27:17

Benefits of Relationships

Every relationship has its own benefits, and these are the fruits/results which God ordained the relationship to bring forth in the earth. The relationship brings strengths and profit to the parties involved in the relationship where and when the proper type and boundaries of fellowship have been followed by all parties involved.

Two are better than one; because they have a good reward for their labour.
For if they fall, the one will lift up his fellow: but woe to him that is alone when hefalleth; for he hath not another to help him up.

Ecclesiastes 4:9-10

Some of the general benefits of relationships are:

1.They multiply strength. Two are better than one therefore, there is always much more achieved through team work or division of labour. Team work produces a greater synergy, as the resultant effect is greater than the mere summation of the individual's strengths or capabilities.

How should one chase a thousand, and two put ten thousand to flight, except their Rock had sold them, and the LORD had shut them up?

Deuteronomy 32:30

2. Through relationships we gain access into the grace of God invested in other men to our advantage. God has not endowed to any one man every resource in this life such that this man can be isolated from all other men. What He has done is that He has made every resource available through different channels to profit us. He has invested some of His wisdom, talents and other strengths in men. When we relate with such people we can benefit from these graces within them. This is so that we can enjoy the gift and grace of God through others (1 Corinthians 12:21-25).

From whom the whole body fitly joined together and <u>compacted by that which every joint supplieth</u>, according to the effectual working in the measure of every part, maketh increase of the body unto the edifying of itself in love.

Ephesians 4:16

3. They help propel us into our God designed destiny. God ordained relationships can quicken or help catalyse our progressive movement into our God designed destiny. Divine relationships when functioning right will always advance us on our journey in our God given purpose.

Thou leddest thy people like a flock by the hand of Moses and Aaron.

Psalm 77:20

Our relationship with God and man

And the scribe said unto him, Well, Master, thou hast said the truth: for there is one God; and thereisnoneother but he:
And to love him with all the heart, and with all the understanding, and with all thesoul, and with all the strength, and to love *his* **neighbour as himself, ismorethan all whole burnt offerings and sacrifices.**

Mark 12:32-33

1. Our vertical relationship with God. This refers to our walk with God, also called our priestly ministry as already discussed in earlier parts of this book. It acts as our fuel station from where we draw God's strengths of wisdom, love, power, etc to be able to carry out our horizontal relationship towards men.

2. Our Horizontal relationship with men. This talks of our human relationships with family, friends, workers, community, etc. We have an earthly ministry to each of the different relationships in this category. This is also were our kingly ministry takes place. We can discover in the scriptures the proper God-ordained fellowship, boundaries, and benefits for each of these different kinds of relationships.

Types of divine relationships with men

There are three scales by which we can categorise our relationships with men:

1. Relationships with seniors. This are the kind of relationships that represent those who God has set in authority above you spiritually, professionally, or socially, so as to aid you get to your destiny. They are accountable to God for your life and have a defined role to play in your destiny. They are appointed and strategically set by God for you and not by man.

They include your pastors and other divinely arranged fivefold ministers (Ephesians 4:11), your parents (if you stay under your parents care), your regional civic government, your seniors at your place of work, etc. Their role is to perfect you and govern you towards the fulfilment of God's designed destiny for you.

This relationship does not encourage superiority (better or more equal than you) but rather seniority (higher position of authority). In order for you to access the strengths of this relationship, you will need to respect and submit to them and their fellowship towards you (whenever this fellowship is in harmony with God's ordained way, boundaries, and righteousness).

2. Peer relationships. Again these are God ordained relationships where God brings you around men and women of certain similarities or contrasts of strengths to spur you on or motivate you. They become companions in destiny's journey. Such was the case of Apostles Paul and Barnabas, who initially were companions in Paul's missionary journeys. The benefit of this relationship is that it inspires you to get to higher heights as they too undertake their own journey into the fullness of God's will for their lives. We see in the Bible numerous examples of this type of relationships including that of Joshua and Caleb, that of the disciples of Jesus Christ, and that of the disciples of John the Baptist.

3. Relationships with juniors. This does not in any way suggest inferiority, but rather those to whom you are more advanced or developed in certain areas of authority, strength, or life. Those in this kind of relationship with you are to draw strength from you and learn from you in these areas of development of life. They are also those who need to gain access into your strengths in order for them to gain speed and direction into their God designed destiny. You are required to serve (Luke 22:25-27) those who relate with you in this fashion and not to lord it over them. A good Biblical example is in the case of Apostle Paul and Timothy.

Safeguarding Divine Relationships

As we engage in these relationships and have our countenance sharpened by that which rubs off from others to us, we must remember that opportunities to take offence or misunderstandings will often arise.

Woe unto the world because of offences! for it must needs be that offences come; but woe to that man by whom the offence cometh!
Matthew 18:7

Offences will cause one to severe links of divine relationships and stop any kind of fellowship within a relationship. This results in an abortion or termination of a God ordained relationship and its benefits. This can further lead to a delay in the fulfilment of God's designed destiny for us. There is a need for wisdom in handling offences and to ensure that God's purpose for that relationship is maintained.

Follow peace with all men, and holiness, without which no man shall see the Lord:
Looking diligently lest any man fail of the grace of God; lest any root of bitterness springing up trouble you, and thereby many be defiled;
Hebrews 12:14-15

The devil takes advantage of our weaknesses in character and our lack of wisdom to make us cause or take offence easily, in order for him (devil) to succeed in terminating a God ordained relationship. We should guard against it and not give place to the devil, by strengthening our character and increasing in wisdom in relating with people.

If it be possible, as much as lieth in you, live peaceably with all men.
Romans 12:18

If you did your best to save or keep a divine relationship, but the other party severed it, then you should be at peace because God will replace the party involved with somebody better. However, if you are the one that severed it, you should repent and mend it quickly; otherwise you may be without such a divine relationship for a while. This will be the case till you have learned to appreciate such God ordained relationships.

TEST YOURSELF
CHAPTER 15 – DIVINE RELATIONSHIPS

The answer sheet is provided at the back of this manual.

1. Which of the following is a benefit of divine relationships?

   a) They multiply our problems as we share with more people.
   b) Through them we gain access into the grace of God invested in other men to our advantage.
   c) They hinder us from being propelled into our God designed destiny.
   d) They cause us to be open to people.

2. Which of the following is true of divine relationships?

   a) Vertical relationships refer to our relationship with men.
   b) They must be discerned and properly cultivated to realise God's will and purposes.
   c) Horizontal relationships refer to our relationship with God.
   d) A divine relationship can never be attacked because it is divine.

3. Which of the following best portrays a peer kind of relationship?

   a) Moses and Joshua.
   b) Paul and Epaphras.
   c) Jesus and the Pharisees.
   d) Paul and Barnabas.

4. In guarding against severing divine relationships we should strengthen our _____and increase in wisdom in relating with people.

5. _____is the strength behind any relationship.

CHAPTER 16:

THE CHURCH AND YOU

The five - fold and the saints

And he gave some, apostles; and some, prophets; and some, evangelists; and some, pastors and teachers;
For the perfecting of the saints, for the work of the ministry, for the edifying of the body of Christ:
Till we all come in the unity of the faith, and of the knowledge of the Son of God, unto a perfect man, unto the measure of the stature of the fulness of Christ:
Ephesians 4:11-13

The five-fold ministry gifts represent a group of ministers within the body of Christ who have been called and positioned by God within the body of Christ for the tasks shown in the above scripture. One does not appoint him or herself into these offices or functions, but is chosen and commissioned by God to carry out these duties.

The five-fold ministry gifts are the gifts of the Apostle, the Prophet, the Evangelist, the Pastor, and the Teacher. They are a set of anointing given to men primarily to help mature, equip, and position the saints into God's fullness or perfection in Christ.

While all the five-fold ministry gifts have their various specialised duties and functions, yet they have been designed and set into the Church by God to collectively fulfil the following in the lives of the believer and the Church at large.

1. They are to bring the believer to full maturity in the **person, glory, and dimensions of Christ**. Colossians 1:28.

2. To bring the saint into a position where the saint can discover, be fully equipped, and execute his or her God given assignment (ministry). 2 Corinthians 5:18-19.

3. To ensure that every mature saint properly contributes his or her strength to the building of the body of Christ through their specialised individual gifting and assignment from God. Ephesians 4:16.

4. This is God's set design for the church through which He will bring the church into unity of faith, the knowledge of the Son of God, a mature man (representing one body) and into the measure of the fullness of the stature of Christ.

5. To govern together with other Elders, the Church of our Lord Jesus Christ on the earth. Hebrews 13:17.

God will keep calling, equipping, and sending the five-fold ministry gifts into the earth and into the body of Christ until these goals are achieved. It is God's design for every saint on the earth to be fathered into their purpose, potential, and inheritance in Christ through the ministry of the five-fold.

The Church

Everyone who has made Jesus Christ their Lord and Saviour through confession with the mouth and believing in the heart has become a child of God and a member of the Body of Christ on the earth. We are now one body with Him. We are all members of this body, yet with different functions within the body.

For as the body is one, and hath many members, and all the members of that one body, being many, are one body: so also is Christ.
For by one Spirit are we all baptized into one body, whether we be Jews or Gentiles, whether we be bond or free; and have been all made to drink into one Spirit.
For the body is not one member, but many.
Now ye are the body of Christ, and members in particular.
1 Corinthians 12:12-14 &27

There are two primary types of churches. These are:

1. The universal church. This is the entire Church of our Lord Jesus Christ made up of believers who have gone to be with the Lord in heaven and believers on the earth. It is made up of both the universal Church in heaven and the universal Church on the earth.

That in the dispensation of the fullness of times he might gather together in one all things in Christ, both which are in heaven, and which are on earth; even in him:
Ephesians 1:10

2. The local church. This is the assembly or gathering of believers (children of God) in a locality such as a city or a building. For example, The Eagles Nest Church, Deliverance Church, All Saints Cathedral, the churches (different assemblies of believers) in Nyeri town, etc.

The churches of Asia salute you. Aquila and Priscilla salute you much in the Lord, with the church that is in their house.
1 Corinthians 16:19

110

We all need to belong not only to the universal Church, but also to a local church, where we can identify with, belong to, and be accountable. The local assembly is what would offer a platform for the work/ministry of the five-fold to be effected in our lives.

Every local church should have **a corporate vision** which aligns with the vision of the universal body of Christ. This corporate vision should work towards fulfilling God's vision towards the individual members of that local church.

Your shepherd

The elders which are among you I exhort, who am also an elder, and a witness ofThe sufferings of Christ, and also a partaker of the glory that shall be revealed: Feed the flock of God which is among you, taking the oversight thereof, not by constraint,but willingly; not for filthy lucre, but of a ready mind; Neither as being lords over God's heritage, but being ensamples to the flock. And when the chief Shepherd shall appear, ye shall receive a crown of glory thatFadeth not away. Likewise, ye younger, submit yourselves unto the elder. Yea, all of you be subjectone to another, and be clothed with humility: for God resisteth the proud, andgiveth grace to the humble. Humble yourselves therefore under the mighty hand of God, that he may exalt you in due time:

1 Peter 5:1-6

Obey them that have the rule over you, and submit yourselves: for they watch forYour souls, as they that must give account, that they may do it with joy, and notwith grief: for that is unprofitable for you.

Hebrews 13:17

Jesus is the Chief Shepherd of His sheep (the believers). He is the one whose blood was shed for the sheep. He paid by His blood for their redemption. They belong to Him and are hence members of His body. Jesus is the head of the entire Universal Church.

The five-fold ministers in charge of a particular local Church are referred to as the **under shepherds** of that congregation of believers. Jesus Christ the Chief Shepherd has given to them the responsibility of administrating the local church, and also to shepherd the believers within that local Church. They act as welfare officers to see to the prosperity of the believer's spirit, soul, body and social life. They are to look to your welfare and your advancement into the purposes, potential, inheritance, and fullness of Christ. They watch over the saint on the Lord's behalf. This is illustrated in the book of Psalms 23, where the shepherd is to feed, protect, guide, comfort, strengthen, refresh, empower, nurture, and nourish the sheep (spiritually, soulically, physically, and socially).

There may be more than one five-fold minister in a local church. It is this team of ministers who now act as your shepherds to bring you through God's word and Spirit into God's fullness for you. They are responsible to also create the church governmental infrastructure which will facilitate these goals.

Your part

You also have a vital part to play in order for the benefits and ministry of the five-fold to take place and become a reality in your life. You must:

1. Locate your own local Church. There is a local Church where you fit in and which. God has ordained for you. You should prayerfully locate it. That means you should pray for God to lead you and help you find the local church best suited for you.

And being let go, they went to <u>their own company</u>, and reported all that the chief priests and elders had said unto them.

Acts 4:23

You should also prove the place. It may not be perfect in everything, but it will be a place conducive for your growth and advancement in Christ. If the church does not make you better in Christ and in the things of Christ, then you should find out why. It might mean either that there is something wrong with you, or that local Church is not your place.

Just like some people have preference for African dishes while others prefer Western or Chinese cuisine, yet they are all good, so it is with the local Church. All local Churches ordained of God are good, but there is one that will fit you best at every stage of your spiritual growth and advancement in Christ.

Sometimes a believer might outgrow a particular local Church and have to move on to another one which God is leading them to. This is comparable to the graduation of a child from primary school to secondary school. This may also be because God wants the person to partake of the strength in another local church in order to mould that person for his or her destiny. This is in order, because God may also want the believer to learn something else in the new local church.

The believer should always make sure that any movement from one local church to another is sincere and not in offence. Any offences should be settled so as not to lead to abortion of purpose. Moving from one Church to the other without genuine reasons is not recommended. It shows a lack of stability in the person. If you have been corrected or rebuked by the under shepherds in one local church and you run to another, you should realise it is the same Kingdom of God you have run to, and that Jesus Christ is still the Chief Shepherd over that local church as well. This means that your refusal to take correction and to relocate from one local assembly to another will not lead to your advancement in life; as you can't break God's righteousness and escape His chastisement just by changing local churches. You need to stay in your local church and go through any biblical correction or rebuke given.

2. Submission for accountability. We need to submit to the under shepherds wherever God plants us. We also should be accountable to them. This is done by our introducing ourselves to the shepherds/leaders of that local church and enrolling in the membership of that Church. When you submit yourself to the leadership in your local Church it is easy for them to watch over you with ease and to do so more effectively.

Obey them that have the rule over you, and submit yourselves: for they watch for your souls, as they that must give account, that they may do it with joy, and not with grief: for that *is* unprofitable for you.

Hebrews 13:17

We not only submit ourselves to Jesus Christ, but we are to also submit ourselves to Church leadership.

And this they did, not as we hoped, but first gave their own selves to the Lord, and unto us by the will of God.

2 Corinthians 8:5

3. Obey them. This allows for easy moulding. As long as the sheep obediently follow the shepherd they will enjoy every benefit and strength of having a shepherd (Psalm 23:1-6). But the sheep that wanders off away from the path the shepherd is leading the sheep in will become exposed to hyenas/wolves (the devourer). It can easily end up in trouble and destruction.

And they rose early in the morning, and went forth into the wilderness of Tekoa: and as they went forth, Jehoshaphat stood and said, Hear me, O Judah, and ye inhabitants of Jerusalem; Believe in the Lord your God, so shall ye be established; believe his prophets, so shall ye prosper.

2 Chronicles 20:20

It is important for the sheep to be close to the shepherd so as to always hear the voice of the shepherd. This means that the sheep must regularly consult with their shepherds (divine five-fold ministers) and be in relevant fellowships/meetings organised by his/her shepherds. Failure to be there means the sheep will miss out of some vital words or information that would take them forward. Members should always catch up on such information if they genuinely have to miss such a meeting. As such information coming from God through the mouth of their under shepherds is vital to their overall prosperity and posterity.

4. Contribution of your strength. The members of a local church should give willingly and freely of their resource (time, gifting, skill, wisdom, and finances) towards the building of the corporate vision of that local church. This will enable the local church to fulfil its God-given mandate on the earth. We are to do this as responsible members of that local body otherwise we can delay the fulfilment of that corporate vision.

And all that believed were together, and had all things common;

Acts 2:44

From whom the whole body fitly joined together and compacted by that which every joint supplieth, according to the effectual working in the measure of every part, maketh increase of the body unto the edifying of itself in love.

Ephesians 4:16

We all have an active part to play in the corporate vision of our local churches. We should remember that the corporate vision of our local churches is designed by God to serve and empower us to become everything that God has ordained for us to be in Him. Therefore any delay in our building and making a reality this corporate vision will ultimately also cause a delay in the fulfilment of our individual purposes and destines in God. We must contribute to make our local church serve us and others better.

Benefits of serving in a church

It is important to pray and meditate about where you can be of service to your local church. Most local churches would have some service groups (some may call them helps ministries, departments, committees, or outreaches, depending on the orientation of the church) where its members can join in voluntary service on a part time basis (maybe on weekday evenings, weekdays, etc).

There are tremendous benefits that come our way when we cease being spectators in a local church and become participators in helping to build the corporate vision. Serving in the different forums in our local churches helps bring about the following benefits:

1. The forums act as centres of training which help to further mature, equip, and launch into position the members of the local church into their own individual, unique, and relevant areas of calling and ministry. They are practical forums for the development and perfection of the saint in Christ likeness (As priests, sons, and kings in God's kingdom).

And he gave some, apostles; and some, prophets; and some, evangelists; and some, pastors and teachers;
For the perfecting of the saints, for the work of the ministry, for the edifying of the body of Christ:
Till we all come in the unity of the faith, and of the knowledge of the Son of God, unto a Perfect man, unto the measure of the stature of the fulness of Christ:

Ephesians 4:11-13

To whom God would make known what is the riches of the glory of this mystery among the Gentiles; which is Christ in you, the hope of glory:
Whom we preach, warning every man, and teaching every man in all wisdom; that we may present every man perfect in Christ Jesus:

Colossians 1:27-28

These forums act as a nursery bed operating under the supervision of the church leaders, whose activities expose the believer to the Kingdom/ministry perspective and dimension of their relevant profession and calling.

2. They help the local Church to strategically and effectively influence the society with its vision.

Go ye therefore, and teach all nations, baptizing them in the name of the Father, and of them Son, and of the Holy Ghost:
Teaching them to observe all things whatsoever I have commanded you: and, lo, I am with Youalway, even unto the end of the world. Amen.
Matthew 28:19-20

And all things are of God, who hath reconciled us to himself by Jesus Christ, and hath given to us the ministry of reconciliation;
To wit, that God was in Christ, reconciling the world unto himself, not imputing theirTrespasses unto them; and hath committed unto us the word of reconciliation.
2 Corinthians 5:18-19

The vision of the local church is strategically made relevant to the different professional, geographical, and language based communities around us, thereby causing us to easily and more effectively reach out to our target world.

3. The specialised contribution of each of these forums helps bring about an excellent ministration to the daily running of the corporate vision of that local church. Realising that when we all work together as a team we are able to accomplish or achieve a more excellent result than any one individual could.

From whom the whole body fitly joined together and compacted by that which every joint supplieth, according to the effectual working in the measure of every part, maketh increase of the body unto the edifying of itself in love.
Ephesians 4:16

And they said one to another, Go to, let us make brick, and burn them thoroughly. And they had brick for stone, and slime had they for mortar.
And they said, Go to, let us build us a city and a tower, whose top may reach untoheaven; and let us make us a name, lest we be scattered abroad upon the face of the whole earth.
And the LORD came down to see the city and the tower, which the children of men builded.
And the LORD said, Behold, the people is one, and they have all one language; and this they begin to do: and now nothing will be restrained from them, which they have imagined to do.
Genesis 11:3-6

4. The forums act as specialised cell groups where people with similar professional skills and gifting within the local church can interact through fellowship, networking, edifying and sharpening one another. It acts as a smaller community within the bigger community of the local church, through which members can be more effectively loved and pastored.

He that walketh with wise men shall be wise: but a companion of fools shall be destroyed.

Proverbs 13:20

And being let go, they went to their own company, and reported all that the chief priests and elders had said unto them.

Acts 4:23

Not forsaking the assembling of ourselves together, as the manner of some is; But exhorting one another: and so much the more, as ye see the day approaching.

Hebrews 10:25

Iron sharpeneth iron; so a man sharpeneth the countenance of his friend.

Proverbs 27:17

TEST YOURSELF
CHAPTER 16 – THE CHURCH AND YOU

The answer sheet is provided at the back of this manual.

1. One of the following scriptures is the correct one. Please tick it.

   a) And he gave some, apostles; and some, prophets; and some, evangelists; and some, pastors and ministers; For the perfecting of the saints, for the work of the ministry, for the edifying of the body of Christ:

   b) And he gave some, apostles; and some, prophets; and some, evangelists; and some, pastors and teachers; For the perfecting of the saints, for the work of the ministry, for the edifying of the body of Christ:

   c) And he gave some, apostles; and some, prophets; and some, evangelists; and some, pastors and teachers; For the perfecting of the saints, for the work of the ministry, for the rebuking of the body of Christ:

   d) And he gave some, apostles; and some, prophets; and some, evangelists; and some, pastors and teachers; For the calling of the saints, for the work of the ministry, for the edifying of the body of Christ:

2. There are two primary types of churches. Which one of the following statements is correct in regard to the two primary types of churches?

   a) THE UNIVERSAL CHURCH: This is the entire church made up of believers who have gone to be with the Lord in heaven, under the earth and believers on the earth. These all make up the universal church in heaven and the universal Church on the earth.

   THE LOCAL CHURCH: This is the assembly or gathering of believers (children of God) in a localisation such as a city or a building.

   b) THE UNIVERSAL CHURCH: This is the entire church made up of believers who have gone to be with the Lord in heaven and believers on the earth. These all make up the universal church in heaven and the universal Church on the earth.

   THE LOCAL CHURCH: This is the assembly or serving of believers (children of God) in a localisation such as a city or a building.

c) THE UNIVERSAL CHURCH: This is the entire church made up of believers who have gone to be with the Lord in heaven and believers on the earth. These all make up the universal church in heaven and the universal Church on the earth.

THE LOCAL CHURCH: This is the assembly or gathering of believers (children of God) in a localisation such as a city or a building.

d) THE UNIVERSAL CHURCH: This is the entire church made up of believers who have gone to be with the Lord in heaven and believers on the earth. These all make up the universal church in heaven and the international Church on the earth.

THE LOCAL CHURCH: This is the assembly or gathering of believers (children of God) in a localisation such as a city or a building.

3. Which of the following is a benefit of serving within a local church?

a) It acts as a forum to train and equip one towards their area of calling.
b) It causes us to be exposed to how church is run so we can start other churches too.
c) It causes the people to be busy in church.
d) It causes us to come into the limelight in church.

4. The_____ in charge of a particular local Church are referred to as the under shepherds of that congregation of believers.

5. The_____of our local churches is designed by God to serve and empower us to become everything that God has ordained for us to be in Him.

TEST YOURSELF

ANSWER SHEETS

TEST YOURSELF – ANSWER SHEET
CHAPTER 1 – THE GODHEAD AND THE FATHER

The correct answers are in bold text and underlined

1. What does the word "Elohiym" mean?

   a) The Lord of Hosts.
   b) **A Supreme Divinity or being.**
   c) The judge of some life forms.
   d) The God who prospers.

2. Who are the Persons that make up the trinity?

   a) The Arch-angels, God the father, and God the Holy Spirit.
   b) God the Word, God the Holy Spirit, and the twenty four elders.
   c) **God the Father, God the Word, and God the Holy Spirit.**
   d) None of the above.

3. Which of the following rightly describes the word Abba?

   a) It is a casual word describing a friend.
   b) It is a name that a servant uses to refer to the master.
   c) **It is an intimate name used by a child to the father.**
   d) None of the above.

4. God the father sits as the head of the **God Head/Trinity.**

5. One of Jesus Christ's roles was to introduce and reveal **God as Father** to mankind.

TEST YOURSELF – ANSWER SHEET
CHAPTER 2 – THE KINGDOM OF GOD

The correct answers are in bold text and underlined

1. What does the word the "Kingdom of God" refer to:

   a) **This is the region, territory, people, geography, resources, and civilization that are under the rule, reign, or influence of God as their King.**
   b) A place in space where the angels live.
   c) Ability to please God in what we do.
   d) The nation of Israel and its tribes.

2. Which one of this sentence best defines Our Kingly ministry:

   a) Our Love unto our Lord.
   b) **Our Service unto the Lord.**
   c) Our sacrifices unto the Lord.
   d) Our Praising unto the Lord.

3. Which one of the following best describes man's purpose on earth:

   a) To buy a Mercedes and become successful.
   b) To climb up to the top of his/her career ladder.
   c) **To worship, reflect, and serve God.**
   d) To become good church members.

4. The kingdom of darkness in its operations can also be referred to as the **world system.**

5. The fulfilment of man's purpose would have him/her function as a priest, a son, and **king.**

TEST YOURSELF – ANSWER SHEET
CHAPTER 3 – RIGHTEOUSNESS

The correct answers are in bold text and underlined

1. Which of the following does not define righteousness?

   a) Right thinking.
   b) **Eating with a fork and a knife.**
   c) Having a right heart.
   d) Walking in divine order.

2. Which of the following statements is not true about righteousness?

   a) God executes and administrates His Kingdom according to His righteousness.
   b) Wherever the righteousness of God is, the Kingdom of God comes into manifestation.
   c) God is Righteous and one of His names is God our Righteousness.
   d) **Righteousness is our own high standards of obeying God.**

3. What is the definition of Holiness?

   a) **Separated from the world and the evil lifestyle that is in it and keeping oneself from the works of the flesh.**
   b) Attending church every Sunday and taking notes.
   c) Singing Holy songs from the Hymn book.
   d) Reading my Bible every day.

4. The word **righteousness** in God's Kingdom means more than just walking in holiness, or even having right standing with God.

5. As a Citizen of God's Kingdom, you belong to God and to **His Kingdom**, and you are to be subject to the laws of that Kingdom.

TEST YOURSELF – ANSWER SHEET
CHAPTER 4 – SALVATION

The correct answers are in bold text and underlined

1. Which Greek word carries the true meaning of the English word "salvation"?

    a) **<u>Soteria</u>**
    b) Christ
    c) Peace
    d) Prosperity

2. The God kind of life is also referred to as?

    a) **<u>Zoe</u>**
    b) Health
    c) Prosperity
    d) Salvation

3. When we are ignorant of God's word, we are ignorant of?

    a) **<u>God's ways</u>**
    b) Good ideas
    c) Our pastors
    d) Good things

4. Salvation makes reference to **<u>total wellness</u>** in every area of life (spirit, soul, and body).

5. One of the major reasons why many believers are not able to enjoy the fullness of salvation is because of **<u>ignorance</u>**.

TEST YOURSELF – ANSWER SHEET
CHAPTER 5 – THE JOURNEY TO SALVATION

The correct answers are in bold text and underlined.

1. Can a person who dies as a Buddhist go to heaven?

    a) Yes, if he/she does a lot of good works.
    b) Yes, if he/she seeks forgiveness from all he/she has ever wronged.
    c) Yes, if he contributes regularly to charity.
    d) **No.**

2. If a wicked, unrighteous, and evil man believes in the sacrifice Jesus Christ paid for him by His death and resurrection, and declares sincerely with his mouth to a friend that Jesus is his Lord and Saviour, would he become born-again?

    a) **Yes.**
    b) No.
    c) Maybe.
    d) Not immediately.

3. Which one of the following does not represent the consequences of man's falling away through sin:

    a) He lost the nature and glory of God.
    b) He brought physical death into the earth and creation.
    c) **He was connected to true fellowship with God.**
    d) He was disconnected from spending eternity with God.

4. When Adam disobeyed God in the garden he lost the **Life** of God also known as Zoe" in the Greek language.

5. God through Jesus Christ's death and resurrection restored man back into God's image and likeness, and back into **oneness**of fellowship with God.

TEST YOURSELF – ANSWER SHEET
CHAPTER 6 – THE DYNAMICS OF MAN

The correct answers are in bold text and underlined

1. The new recreated man whose spirit is restored back to God is one who:

    a. Looks different from others.
    b. Portrays good habits to his/her community.
    c. Goes to church and reads the word.
    d. **Has God dwelling in Him as His temple.**

2. The part of man that has God consciousness and is in touch with spiritual realities is:

    a) **The spirit.**
    b) The body.
    c) The feelings.
    d) The soul.

3. The self-conscious part of man is his:

    a) Spirit.
    b) Body.
    c) Temperament.
    d) **Soul.**

4. Man's soul does not get saved instantly at salvation and must therefore undergo three processes in order to effect the purpose of salvation of the soul. They are the **renewing of the mind**, submitting of the will, and taming of the emotions.

5. Man's **body** is the casing that gives him legal grounds to operate and function on the earth.

TEST YOURSELF – ANSWER SHEET
CHAPTER 7 – THE NEW CREATION

The correct answers are in bold text and underlined

1. We become new creatures:

   a) At biological birth.
   b) At resurrection.
   c) **When we get born again.**
   d) When we do many good works.

2. Which of the following is a reality of becoming a new creature?

   a) We are changed from the outside in.
   b) **We are changed from the inside out.**
   c) We receive a new life after some years in the Lord.
   d) We lose touch of this world and become funny people.

3. Which of the following is true concerning the name "Christ"?

   a) It was the surname of Jesus.
   b) **It refers to the anointed one and His anointing.**
   c) It is the name given by the angel to Elizabeth, Mary's cousin.
   d) None of the above.

4. The reality of Christ in you becomes the **glory** of this new creature.

5. It is the new creature called **Christ** within you that God will use to demonstrate His glory and purposes unto the inhabitants of the earth.

TEST YOURSELF – ANSWER SHEET
CHAPTER 8 – PURPOSE

The correct answers are in bold text and underlined

1. Every creation of God was created for a purpose which is:

    a) To enjoy life.
    b) To become famous.
    c) **To fulfil God's will and pleasure.**
    d) To have riches.

2. We find out the true purpose of our lives by:

    a) Asking other people.
    b) **Spending time with God.**
    c) Attending seminars.
    d) Reading books.

3. Which one of the following does not make reference to the term nations?

    a) People called to a particular community.
    b) People who share a common industry or profession.
    c) People who share a common geographical boundary.
    d) **People who share similar views in life.**

4. The term vision means **God given insight into God's purposes for your life**.

5. God never sends a person on a divine assignment without first **equipping**the person with the ability to carry out the divine task at hand.

TEST YOURSELF- ANSWER SHEET
CHAPTER 9 - THE WORD OF GOD

The correct answers are in bold text and underlined

1. The word of God is profitable to us in the following ways. Which one is not true?

   a) It establishes us in sound doctrine.
   b) For correction.
   c) For instruction in righteousness.
   d) **It tells us that we shall live in heaven forever after life on earth.**

2. The following statements are not true about how holy men came up with scriptures. Which one is true?

   a) The holy men discovered where the scriptures had been hidden by God.
   b) The Holy Ghost was inspired by holy men to write scriptures.
   c) Holy men through research found out about God and they put it in writing.
   d) **The holy men were inspired by the Holy Ghost to write the scriptures.**

3. Which of the following is not true concerning the word?

   a) It is Jesus Christ personified.
   b) It was the instrument that was used in the creation process.
   c) It is what man is to be continually sustained by and not by bread alone.
   d) **It is what was written by men who had a religious experience.**

4. Without discovering and **applying** the word of God into our lives, our lives will not reflect any added value.

5. The word of God carries **transforming power** for every area of our lives thus making it relevant in every stage and point in life.

TEST YOURSELF- ANSWER SHEET
CHAPTER 10 – THE HOLY SPIRIT

The correct answers are in bold text and underlined

1. Whichof the following is true about who the Holy Spirit is?

   a) A wind.
   b) A fire.
   c) A feeling.
   d) <u>The third person of the trinity.</u>

2. The Holy Spirit is our Parakletos. Which of the following is not His role as Parakletos?

   a) A guide.
   b) A teacher.
   c) <u>A prophet.</u>
   d) A counsellor.

3. Which of the following is a proper definition of the fruit of the Spirit?

   a) **<u>It is the character or nature of God given by and through the Holy Spirit to men.</u>**
   b) It is recommendable behaviours in a people.
   c) It is the equivalent of behavioural temperaments in people.
   d) It is the mastering of good traits from proper upbringing.

4. The five-fold ministry gifts are **<u>apostle</u>**, prophet, evangelist, pastor, and teacher.

5. There are **<u>nine</u>** manifestations (gifts) the Holy Spirit as recorded in the Bible.

TEST YOURSELF – ANSWER SHEET
CHAPTER 11 – THE HOLY SPIRIT

The correct answers are in bold text and underlined

1. Which of the following statements about the Holy Spirit is not true?

    a) The Holy Spirit comes to dwell in a person immediately after he/she becomes born again.
    b) **There are numerous instances in scriptures where people got baptised with the Holy Ghost and then saved later.**
    c) Jesus spoke of the experience of baptism of the Holy spirit as an infilling of the Holy Ghost.
    d) One of the evidence of the baptism of the Holy Ghost in the life of a believer is speaking with new tongues.

2. Praying in tongues can be described in all of the following ways except?

    a) It is a heavenly language.
    b) It is an experience of praying in unknown tongue.
    c) It is a language.
    d) **It is part of the human languages.**

3. Which one of the following is a benefit of baptism of the Holy Spirit?

    a) It causes us to become spiritually funny people.
    b) **It enables us to live in God's power and manifest Christ wherever we are.**
    c) It makes us viable to become church leaders.
    d) It causes us to speak in strange languages that we are not sure of.

4. The Holy Spirit comes to help us in our **limitations** because there are situations where we may not know or be unsure of the will of God.

5. It takes **faith** to receive the baptism of the Holy Spirit as the answer to Galatians 3:2 and Galatians 3:5 indicate.

TEST YOURSELF – ANSWER SHEET
CHAPTER 12 – WORSHIP AND PRAISE

The correct answers are in bold text and underlined

1. Which of the following statements about praise is not true?

   a) It serves to help build intimacy with God.
   b) **It is the only mode of worship that evokes God to act on our behalf.**
   c) It activates the hand and blessings of God on our favour.
   d) It invokes God to act on our behalf.

2. Worship can be defined in all of the following ways except:

   a) The aspect of the worth of something or someone.
   b) Worship translates into whatever we do or engage ourselves in that givesGod His value in our lives.
   c) It is our expression of God's worth or value due to Him.
   d) **It portrays only singing slow songs**.

3. Which of the following is true about the purpose of praise?

   a) **It helps to build our intimacy with God.**
   b) It is a strategy to help us lose weight through dancing.
   c) The faster the praise song the better the mood.
   d) It is what we do to prepare us to worship God in spirit and in truth.

4. Praise must be offered from a **heart of worship**towards God.

5. Praise can be very **dynamic**and wholesome when we involve our spirit, our soul and our body.

TEST YOURSELF – ANSWER SHEET
CHAPTER 13 – PRAYER

The correct answers are in bold text and underlined

1. As a priest unto God a believer must know how to commune with God through:

   a) Serving others in church.
   b) **Prayer.**
   c) Attending the church service early Sunday morning.
   d) Clapping their hands unto God.

2. Prayer can be defined in all of the following ways except:

   a) The art of communication between a believer and God through prayer.
   b) It is man communing with God.
   c) Prayer is simply communicating with God.
   d) **Giving God his due.**

3. Which one of the following describes the purposes of prayer?

   a) It is an avenue to express our complaints to God.
   b) It is an exercise we do to fulfill Christian obligation.
   c) **It is an avenue to develop intimate fellowship with God.**
   d) It is where we confess and possess what we want.

4. It is important that we learn that prayer must be backed by a lifestyle of **righteousness**.

5. A prayer backed by **gratitude** is a prayer offered in faith.

TEST YOURSELF – ANSWER SHEET
CHAPTER 14 – LOVE

The correct answers are in bold text and underlined

1. Which of the following is not true about love?

    a) We are commanded by God to love all fellow believers.
    b) Most important of all we are to love the Lord God Almighty.
    c) In scripture the word love has many meanings.
    d) **The love of God is the only type of love we have**.

2. What is true about walking in love?

    a) All born again believers lack the ability to walk in agape.
    b) The love of God has been put in our hearts by our maturity.
    c) **We need to walk in Agape towards all men**.
    d) All of the above.

3. Which of the following is a type of love?

    a) **Storge**.
    b) Feeling.
    c) Emotions.
    d) Thoughts.

4. Agape is a type of love that **that has no conditions to it**

5. **Eros** is the love that should be exchanged only between a husband and his wife.

TEST YOURSELF – ANSWER SHEET
CHAPTER 15 – DIVINE RELATIONSHIPS

The correct answers are in bold text and underlined

1. Which of the following is a benefit of divine relationships?

   a) They multiply our problems as we share with more people.
   b) **Through them we gain access into the grace of God invested in other men to our advantage**.
   c) They hinder us from being propelled into our God designed destiny.
   d) They cause us to be open to people.

2. Which of the following is true of divine relationships?

   a) Vertical relationships refer to our relationship with men.
   b) **They must be discerned and properly cultivated to realise God's will and purposes.**
   c) Horizontal relationships refer to our relationship with God.
   d) A divine relationship can never be attacked because it is divine.

3. Which of the following best portrays a peer kind of relationship?

   a) Moses and Joshua.
   b) Paul and Epaphras.
   c) Jesus and the Pharisees.
   d) **Paul and Barnabas.**

4. In guarding against severing divine relationships we should strengthen our **character** and increase in wisdom in relating with people.

5. **Fellowship** is the strength behind any relationship.

TEST YOURSELF – ANSWER SHEET
CHAPTER 16 – THE CHURCH AND YOU

The correct answers are in bold text and underlined

1. One of the following scriptures is the correct one. Please tick it.

   a) And he gave some, apostles; and some, prophets; and some, evangelists; and some, pastors and ministers; For the perfecting of the saints, for the work of the ministry, for the edifying of the body of Christ:

   b) **<u>And he gave some, apostles; and some, prophets; and some, evangelists; and some, pastors and teachers; For the perfecting of the saints, for the work of the ministry, for the edifying of the body of Christ:</u>**

   c) And he gave some, apostles; and some, prophets; and some, evangelists; and some, pastors and teachers; For the perfecting of the saints, for the work of the ministry, for the rebuking of the body of Christ:

   d) And he gave some, apostles; and some, prophets; and some, evangelists; and some, pastors and teachers; For the calling of the saints, for the work of the ministry, for the edifying of the body of Christ:

2. There are two primary types of churches. Which one of the following statements is correct in regard to the two primary types of churches?

   a) THE UNIVERSAL CHURCH: This is the entire church made up of believers who have gone to be with the Lord in heaven, under the earth and believers on the earth. These all make up the universal church in heaven and the universal Church on the earth.

   THE LOCAL CHURCH: This is the assembly or gathering of believers (children of God) in a localisation such as a city or a building.

   b) THE UNIVERSAL CHURCH: This is the entire church made up of believers who have gone to be with the Lord in heaven and believers on the earth. These all make up the universal church in heaven and the universal Church on the earth.

   THE LOCAL CHURCH: This is the assembly or serving of believers (children of God) in a localisation such as a city or a building.

c) **THE UNIVERSAL CHURCH: This is the entire church made up of believers who have gone to be with the Lord in heaven and believers on the earth. These all make up the universal church in heaven and the universal Church on the earth.**

THE LOCAL CHURCH: This is the assembly or gathering of believers (children of God) in a localisation such as a city or a building.

d) THE UNIVERSAL CHURCH: This is the entire church made up of believers who have gone to be with the Lord in heaven and believers on the earth. These all make up the universal church in heaven and the international Church on the earth.

THE LOCAL CHURCH: This is the assembly or gathering of believers (children of God) in a localisation such as a city or a building.

3. Which of the following is a benefit of serving within a local church?

   a) **It acts as a forum to train and equip one towards their area of calling.**
   b) It causes us to be exposed to how church is run so we can start other churches too.
   c) It causes the people to be busy in church.
   d) It causes us to come into the limelight in church.

4. The **Five fold** ministries in charge of a particular local Church are referred to as the under shepherds of that congregation of believers.

5. The **corporate vision** of our local churches is designed by God to serve and empower us to become everything that God has ordained for us to be in Him.

HOW TO BECOME A CHILD OF GOD

AND A CITIZEN OF GOD'S KINGDOM

Would you like to become a child of God, a member of God's own household, and a citizen of God's Kingdom? If your answer is yes, then all you have to do is to follow the simple step of reading out with your mouth the "prayer of salvation" written below, at the same time believing in it with your whole heart (Romans 10:9-10).

You might not have any sensational feeling, and you don't have to have one. But a transformation will take place immediately in your spirit man. Your spirit man will be regenerated and become a new creature in Christ Jesus. This is what it means to be born again: you are reborn on the inside into the exact image and likeness of God and of Christ Jesus as taught in this book.

After this prayer continue to study and apply the truths in the Christian Bible. Join a Bible-believing and practicing Church. This will help you to mature and be better equipped in Christ, and in the Kingdom of God. As you remain consistent in doing these you will grow in maturity as a believer.

Prayer of salvation

Dear heavenly Father, I come before you this day, believing in my heart that Jesus Christ died for me, that you raised Him up from the dead, and that He is alive and well.

I believe in my heart and confess with my mouth that Jesus Christ is my personal Lord and Saviour from this moment forward. Wash me with the precious blood of Jesus Christ and forgive me for all my sins.

I am now your son, a child of God, and a citizen of your great Kingdom. From now on you are my Father, my God, and my friend. Teach me to worship, reflect, and serve you.

Thank you Father, thank you my Lord Christ Jesus, and thank you Holy Spirit. In Jesus name I pray.

Karibu (welcome) to God's family

If you just said this prayer, welcome to God's family. You are now a child of the Most High God.

THE JOSHUA GENERATION

The Joshua Generation is a Christian Missionary organisation and a Christian Community. It is registered as a Christian religious trust and headquartered in Nairobi, Kenya.

The vision of The Joshua Generation is taken from the book of Joshua, in the Christian Bible.

Our goal is to mature, equip, and rightly position the born again believers in Christ, empowering them to cross over their Jordan (any obstacle or hindrance, internally or externally that stands in their path), and enable them to see, enter into, possess, and maintain their Promised Land.

The Promised Land being the believer's God-ordained purpose in life; the fullness of their spiritual, soulical, and physical potential; and every promise or prophecy of blessing and inheritance for the believer in Christ Jesus. Therefore bringing the believers into their full maturity, equipping, and positioning as Priests, Sons (Kingdom fathers), and Kings in God's Kingdom. This will help establish the reality of God's will and Kingdom both in the life of the believer, the unbeliever, and over the earth (Matthew 28:18-20).

We summarise this by saying, **"Our vision is to make your God given vision a reality"**.

The major goals of the ministry as deduced from the vision are:

a. To perfect (mature and equip) the born again believers in Christ.

b. To empower the born again believer to cross over their Jordan (any obstacle or hindrance, internally or externally that stands in their path).

c. To enable the born again believer to see, enter into, possess, and maintain their Promised Land (this is the believer's God-ordained purpose in life; the fullness of their spiritual, soulical, and physical potential; and every promise or prophecy of blessing and inheritance for the believer in Christ Jesus).

d. To bring the believers into their full maturity, equipping, and positioning as Priests, Sons (Kingdom fathers), and Kings in God's Kingdom.

e. To help establish the reality of God's will both in the life of the believer and on the earth (Matthew 6:10 & Luke 22:42).

f. To help establish God's Kingdom over the believers, the nations (communities, civilizations, geography, and resource), and over the entire earth (Matthew 6:10, 2 Corinthians 5:18-19, & Matthew 28:18-20).

THE KINGDOM ACADEMY

The Kingdom Academy is the school of Ministry of the Joshua Generation. Every believer has a mandate to establish the Kingdom of God on the earth. The Kingdom Academy is a school established by the Joshua Generation to equip the born again believer for this mandate.

The school is designed according to the pattern used by Jesus Christ to train His disciples during His three and a half years of ministry on the earth. The school is set to Kingdom and international standards. Students are equipped with a wealth of knowledge and understanding that is both relevant and readily applicable.

We believe that every human being is called to one or more of the seven professional nations/mountains/spheres/cultures/worlds of calling. The school raises the students to be effective Priests, Sons and Kings: to worship, reflect and serve God in his/her profession area of calling. The Kingdom Academy imparts to the believer principles that help him/her discover his/herprofessionalnation of calling and how to use it as their pulpit to execute this Kingdom mandate.

The school curriculum hosts ten courses that are taught in a period of two years. It includes, Theory Classes – where Kingdom Principles are taught with clarity, Practical Exercises assigned to each course, Character Building exercises, and Practical Ministry Projects (PMPs) – where students are sent out in groups to executive a major practical project (one per year) that will make demand on them to apply the lessons taught in class.

The syllabus of the school includes the following ten courses outlined in the order they are taught, each course being a foundation for the next:

The Godhead

This unit deals with the teachings about God; the course has been compiled to help the student receive accurate knowledge and understanding of who God is, His attributes, and His functions. Some of the topics Covered in this course include: - Theology, Ministry of the Father, Ministry of the Son, and the Ministry of The Holy Spirit.

The Bible

The Bible is the Word of God and a manual for proper human existence. The subject of this course is to understand the authenticity of the Bible, its accurate interpretation, and how to rightly apply the Kingdom principles found in it towards the God-kind of success in this life. Some of these topics covered in this course include:- The Bible as a library, Compilation and Canonization, Bible History, Old and New Testament Survey, Ancient Kingdoms and Cultures, Types and Shadows, Places of Worship and The Study of the Bible.

The Kingdom of God

Every Kingdom is governed by a King and functions according to its set order. Having already known the King of this Kingdom and His delegated kings, this unit introduces the student to the principles and order that govern His Kingdom.

The purpose of this course is to help the student learn to live a life of divine order, and rightly propagate the advancement of the Kingdom of God. Some of the topics covered include: The Kingdom defined, The History of God's Kingdom Dispensations, The Kingdom Community, Benefits of the Kingdom, A Kingdom of Righteousness, Angels, Enemies of God's Kingdom, Kingdom Technology, Technology for Manifesting in the Holy Ghost, and The Kingdom Technician.

Salvation

From the fall of Adam, a ridge has existed between God and Man. Jesus Christ came to bridge this gap and restore man into the glory of God. This course is designed to bring the students to an understanding of the total package of salvation and to shed light on how they can appropriate it in their lives. Some of the Topics covered in this course include: - The Fall of Man, The Need for Salvation, Understanding Salvation (Soteria), the Journey to Salvation, The study of Religion/Worldviews, Evangelism, Principles/Technology of Salvation, and Christian Counselling.

New Creation Realities

This course brings the student to an understanding of The New Testament Man, and how God intended him to live in this day and age. It re-awakens him to the inexhaustible resources within this New Creation. Some of the topics covered in this course include: The Origin and Creation of Man, The Fall and Regeneration of Man, The Nature and types of Man, Dynamics of Man, an In-depth analysis of the Human Spirit, Soul and Body, the Ministries of Man, and Healing from predispositions.

New Testament Doctrine

This course examines the basic teachings of the Word of God. It seeks to de-mystify doctrines and teachings previously assumed as preserve of the clergy. The student gains a hands-on understanding of the basic foundational teachings of the New Testament and its application in their daily lives. Some of the Topics covered in this course includes: - Understanding Doctrines, Worship and Praise, Payer, Faith, Communion & Baptisms, Giving, Laying of Hands, and Eschatology.

Your Kingly Ministry

Every saint has a calling as a King to influence and impact his/her professional, geographical, and language-based world with the Kingdom of God. This jurisdiction is their environment of optimum performance. This course explores the parameters and the dynamics of the saint's Kingly Ministry, and teaches the student to be successful at it. Some of the Topics covered in this course include:- The Business of the Kingdom, The Believer as King, Purpose and Ministry, Diversity and Specialised Ministry (to the Seven Professional Nations/Mountains), Ministry Building Technology/principles, Kingdom/Ministry Ethics, Women in Ministry, Cross Cultural Ministry, Effective Kingdom Ministration, Marriage and the Family, Divine Relationships, Social Etiquette, and Reconciling your Nation to God.

Your Priestly Ministry

"Every strong King must have a strong Priest". The King who understands and walks in this principle stands a better chance of success than the one who doesn't. Every believer is both a Priest and a King, therefore any weakness in a person's priestly office is an automatic set up for failure in the person's Kingly Ministry. Some of the topics covered in this course include: - Understanding the Office of a Priest, The believer as a Priest, The KingPriest,Hearing and Walking with God as a Priest, Sacrifices of a Priest, Mastering the Office of the Priest, Inception and Progression of the Priestly Office, and Transcending Glories.

New Testament Church

Every believer on the Earth forms part of the Body of Christ, beginning from the local assembly to a worldwide corporate body. In this course the students learn about the purpose, the structure and the mandate of the Church of Jesus Christ. Some of the topics covered in this course include: - God's purpose for the Church, Kingdom/Church Government, Kingdom Patterns-Structures-Forums-Systems, Kingdom Offices and Pillars, Five-fold Ministry Gifts, Fatherhood, Kingdom/Church Administration, Church History and Perfection, Kenyan Church History, and Transcending Dispensations.

Kingdom Business

Every believer in Christ should handle his/her assignment/ministry as the Lord's Business. Kingdom Business educates the student on how to start, build and establish his/her ministry as a successful kingdom enterprise. This course introduces the saint to basic Business principles that will help him/her to achieve this purpose. Some of the topics covered in this course include:- Kingdom Business, Industry and Technology, Human Resource, Kingdom Leadership, Communication, Strategic Planning and Policy Making, Marketing and Sales, Media Communication, Financial Management, Business Report Writing, and Business Law.

THE JOSHUA GENERATION
WEBSITE RESOURCE PAGE

(Books, Literature, Audio Material)

For any other Resources, Books, Literature, Video, Audio Messages from the Joshua Generation use the following link:

http://thejoshuagenerationtrust.org/pages/resources.html

The Joshua Generation Trust ☑ jgmediatrust, jgmediachannel

www.thejoshuagenerationtrust.org

MAIN CONTRIBUTORS

All the Contributors to this Volume/Book are past or present members of the Kingdom Academy (the school of ministry of the Joshua Generation Trust) faculty and of The Joshua Generation Trust Nairobi, Kenya.

www.ingramcontent.com/pod-product-compliance
Lightning Source LLC
LaVergne TN
LVHW081333060426

835513LV00014B/1272